"According to Proverbs 13:20, 'He who walks with the wise will grow wise.' I've walked with Boyd Bailey for more than 28 years, and I'm definitely wiser for it. I've followed Boyd in his role as husband, father, leader, pastor, and friend. His success in each of these roles reflects his relentless pursuit and application in the very things he writes about: wisdom. You're going to love this book!"

Andy Stanley, North Point Ministries

"I have known Boyd Bailey for years, and I have long considered him a man of great wisdom and superb counsel. When I heard that he was writing a book about leadership—specifically about leadership as lived and taught by Jesus—I was thrilled. I knew it would be a must read. And sure enough, it is! Deeply based in Scripture and chock full of personal stories and examples, this book provides tremendous insight and instruction to anyone seeking to be a wise leader, one who strives to lead as God would have him(or her) do it. If you want to motivate and develop your people in a way that encourages and challenges them to give their best—for themselves, for your organization, and for God— read this book!"

Paul Trotti, Colonel, US Army (Ret.) and president, To the Top Leadership, LLC

"We have all read many books on leadership, and we at times still sense a gap in leading well. Boyd has written a masterful book, leading us to the one true example and guide, Jesus! This book is a treasure and one that I will reread. It gave me new insights and a deeper understanding regarding the wisdom of leading myself and others well. Thank you, Boyd."

Dan Glaze, National Christian Foundation, National Relationship Manager

"Boyd's book contains more than principles or the typical to-do list. It contains useful and meaningful truth on acquiring and applying wisdom in leadership. I learned that wisdom is better than wealth, more than a wish, is available and waiting, we find it where we walk, and above all, wisdom works! We can ask for it, pursue it, receive it, and grow in it. It is a blessing to not be missed. I highly recommend this for your reading list."

Randy Thrasher, National Christian Foundation,
Chief Operating Officer

"I am so pleased to call myself a friend of Boyd. This book is right on! Boyd outlines with moving clarity timeless principles that are inspirational for the twenty-first century leader."

David Deeter, CPA, Fraizer-Deeter

"I've appreciated Boyd's wisdom for a number of years, and this latest book is something that's needed for all of us desiring to lead wisely. I'm intrigued that no one to my knowledge has written a book with a complete perspective about wisdom in leadership. Stories are wonderful ways to illustrate principles, and I love how Boyd has shared stories from his personal journey, which bring the principles to life!"

Bill Williams, Haggai Institute

"For years now one of my morning's first reads is that of Boyd Bailey. Wisdom Hunters is an appropriate name for one so full of our Lord's wisdom. Read *Learning to Lead Like Jesus* and you will see."

Johnny Hunt, pastor, First Baptist Woodstock, Georgia

"My favorite verse on leadership is Psalm 78:72: 'David shepherded them with integrity of heart; with skillful hands he led them.' The qualities of the heart and the hands are of equal importance in leadership. Boyd has, over many years, demonstrated both in his life, his family, and his profession. In this book Boyd insightfully communicates the heart and hand qualities that reflect how Jesus led—qualities that, if incorporated into our lives, can transform our leadership skills."

Shane Williamson, president and CEO, FCA

"I am always on the hunt for leadership truths that are both timely and timeless; principles that are relevant for the moment in which we live and that work wherever we go. This is what Boyd Bailey has offered to us in this book. As you read it, you'll find sound wisdom you can practice today. The insights are a reflection of Boyd's life. I recommend this book to you."

Tim Elmore, founder, GrowingLeaders.com

"Several years ago we acknowledged that the success of our family of companies would rise and fall on leadership, and we therefore needed to be intentional about being green and growing or we would become ripe and rotting. Boyd's book is a blueprint for all of us to follow and learn from in that we should lead like Jesus. Leading like Jesus will allow you to have the greatest impact on your company, clients, partners, staff, and friends. The book is one you will share and reread often and a blessing not to be missed."

Jimmy Rousey, CEO, Family of Companies /
First Southern Bancorp / UTG

"Jesus trained twelve men who went on to influence the world. In so doing, He taught them to recognize their own human weaknesses. Despite these struggles, He taught them to lead. Boyd breaks down the traits Jesus valued most in a leader. His writings continue to evoke spiritual energy with his insights and storytelling. These principles are as pertinent today as they were 2000 years ago. This a book that is a 'forever resource' on leadership. Proverbs 2:6: 'The LORD gives wisdom; from his mouth come knowledge and understanding.'"

Jack McEntee, retired CEO, Nth Degree

"Boyd is a follower and a student of Jesus. He has taken the leadership principles Jesus taught and put them into a must-read book on leadership. I have spent time with Boyd and watched and learned how he applies these principles as a servant leader in his family, ministry, and business. Boyd, thank you for the impact you have had on my life."

Sonny Newton, retired Chick-fil-A executive

"You will not find a book on leadership like this one. Every page is infused with authenticity as Boyd shares from a lifetime of not merely seeking or accumulating wisdom, but resolutely and consistently striving to apply it in every area of life. So this is not a book to rush through. Read it slowly and prayerfully. Your relationships with our Master and with those closest to you will never be the same."

Doug Ditto, chief investment officer,
First Southern National Bank

"James 1:5 states, 'If any of you lacks wisdom, you should ask God... and it will be given to you.' If you are seeking wisdom in how to lead, ask God for wisdom, and see what He shows you in these pages from Boyd Bailey."

Cliff Robinson, vice president of operations,
Chick-fil-A

"As a young leader I desired to surround myself with previous-generation wisdom walkers. For several years I heard about a man named Boyd Bailey and began watching the significant impact his mentorship was having on young leaders around me. It became my desire to someday be one of the lucky few who would be graced by personal encounters with him. Eventually that hope became a reality as Boyd began a personal mentorship of myself and the board of directors from the K-12 school that I was leading. Many will speak about wisdom, but few will actually live out those life-giving principles. Boyd Bailey is a man who both speaks and walks in the ways of wisdom because he speaks and walks in the ways of our Savior Jesus Christ, this Jesus who 'has become for us wisdom sent from God.' Oh that everyone would be so blessed as to hear Boyd's understanding and voice of wisdom. *Learning to Lead Like Jesus* makes that possible."

Daniel Cline, vice president of partnership,
Catalyst Conferences

"Look no further than the introduction of this excellent book to help you know if it is worth your time to read it. Ask yourself this three-part question: Do you 'desperately need the Holy Spirit's direction, the Father's wisdom, and the Son's encouragement'? Well, if that's you, then this book will be like a breath of fresh air and a cool drink of water to your soul. I have read the whole thing cover to cover and it looks like I've gone through several highlighters! I think I have read most all of Boyd's previous works—this is his best...so far! My recommendation is to not read this alone and not read it straight through. Take one chapter at a time and chew on it for a while—this is more like a smorgasbord than a book. This book is full of truth and it will give you direction, wisdom, and encouragement. So get a friend or two to join you, pull up a chair, grab a cup of coffee, and enjoy *Learning to Lead Like Jesus*."

David Wills, National Christian Foundation

"I wholeheartedly believe there has never been a greater leadership role model than Jesus. In *Learning to Lead Like Jesus*, Boyd Bailey amplifies the qualities of Christ in a way that challenges, but also encourages you to see what is possible in your own leadership. Through the pages of Scripture and how others have followed Christ's leadership example, you'll discover your potential to do the same!"

Tami Heim, president and CEO,
Christian Leadership Alliance

LEARNING
TO
LEAD
LIKE
JESUS

BOYD BAILEY

HARVEST HOUSE PUBLISHERS
EUGENE, OREGON

Learning to Lead Like Jesus

Copyright © 2018 by Boyd Bailey
Published by Harvest House Publishers
Eugene, Oregon 97408
www.harvesthousepublishers.com

ISBN 978-0-7369-7244-4 (pbk.)
ISBN 978-0-7369-7245-1 (eBook)

Library of Congress Cataloging-in-Publication Data

Names: Bailey, Boyd, 1960- author.
Title: Learning to lead like Jesus / Boyd Bailey.
Description: Eugene, Oregon : Harvest House Publishers, 2018.
Identifiers: LCCN 2017059567 (print) | LCCN 2018006833 (ebook) | ISBN 9780736972451 (ebook) | ISBN 9780736972444 (pbk.)
Subjects: LCSH: Jesus Christ—Example. | Leadership—Religious aspects—Christianity.
Classification: LCC BT304.2 (ebook) | LCC BT304.2 .B35 2018 (print) | DDC 253—dc23
LC record available at https://lccn.loc.gov/2017059567

7/2/18

Ryn,

Love

To my friend Randy Thrasher, who models leading like Jesus and challenges me and many others to do the same.

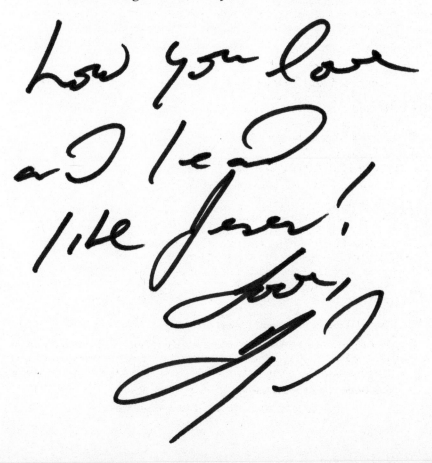

how you love
and lead
like Jesus!

Acknowledgments

A special thanks to Paul Trotti Sr., a man's man who likes doing manly things and loves Jesus! I admire your service to God and country with the 82nd Airborne Division in Panama and Desert Storm, and your investment in West Point cadets as an ethics professor, while being a skilled editor. The Lord used you to bring me clarity when these pages were but a fog—Sir, yes sir!

A shout-out to Andy Stanley, my friend and pastor, who inspires and instructs me in learning to lead like Jesus.

Thank you Wisdom Hunters team for loving like Jesus: Rita Bailey, Bethany Thoms, Gwynne Mauffet, Shanna Schutte, Rachel Snead, Rachel Prince, Tripp Prince, Susan Fox, and Josh Randolph.

Thank you National Christian Foundation for the opportunity to reach and restore every person through the love of Christ, and to mobilize resources by inspiring biblical generosity.

I am grateful to our community group for keeping it real! Life is twice as blessed and half as hard because of you: Betsy and Bill Chapman, Alison and Bill Ibsen, Aria and Josh Randolph, Jodi and Andy Ward, and, best of all, my sweetheart Rita Isbill Bailey.

Finishing Well accountability guys, thanks for deep "scuba diving" conversations instead of shallow "snorkeling" small talk: Frank Bell, Woody Faulk, Mike Kendrick, and Scotland Wright.

Book clubs, you are the best. Morning: David Deeter, Nathan Deeter, and Mike Davis. Classics: Larry Green, Bill Ibsen, and Bill Williams. Virtual: Dan Brown, Greg James, and Greg Mauldin.

I am grateful to our family for being such a support: Rita, Rebekah, Todd, Hudson, Harrison, Marshall, Rachel, Tripp, Lily, Emmie, Charlie, Bethany, J.T., Weston, Anna, and Tyler.

Thank you Paul Trotti, Susan Fox, and Michael Jaffarian for your expert editing.

Thank you Wisdom Hunters board of directors for your love, prayers, and accountability: Cliff Bartow, Andrew Wexler, and John Hightower. Advisors: Debbie Ochs and Cliff Bartow.

Thank you Harvest House Publishers for your vision and support for this book: Bob Hawkins, Aaron Dillon, Gene Skinner, Terry Glaspey, Ken Lorenz, Kathy Zemper, and Brad Moses.

Most of all I am grateful to Jesus, from whom I am learning to lead.

Contents

Foreword

In nearly 40 years of management, I have met all types of leaders. From those who crave the spotlight to those who let others shine. When I became CEO of Popeyes Louisiana Kitchen, Inc., I set out to role model and teach a different kind of leadership. The secret I uncovered and share in my book, *Dare to Serve*, is that the most remarkable leaders are "*courageous* enough to take the people to a daring destination, yet *humble* enough to selflessly serve others on the journey."

Boyd Bailey is that kind of leader.

In *Learning to Lead Like Jesus*, Boyd explores the 11 character traits that make Jesus the gold standard for servant leadership, starting with humility. His engaging storytelling and relevant teaching point the reader to Jesus's model of leadership through service.

Boyd's authority to equip readers to follow Jesus's footsteps comes from his own humble service and a day-by-day commitment to live his life dedicated to following Christ.

There is no better time than now to choose to serve humbly and lead courageously to impact your relationships, your family, your company, your city, and your world.

Cheryl Bachelder
Former CEO of Popeyes Louisiana Kitchen, Inc.

Introduction:
Where True Leadership Begins

Learning to lead like Jesus is a lifetime journey that begins with humility. "It's better to say, 'I am learning,' than to say, 'I have learned,'"—wise and humble words indeed from Dr. Charles Stanley, spoken to me and several staff members at First Baptist of Atlanta in the late 1980s. When I was a young pastor, this seasoned leader helped me understand how to follow the Lord Jesus by continuing to learn and grow. For example, don't say, "I've learned to be a patient leader." Say, "I'm learning to be a patient leader." This reminds me to be a humble, teachable, and ever-growing leader who is always in desperate need of God's grace.

This book is for leaders who, like me, desperately need the Holy Spirit's direction, the Father's wisdom, and the Son's encouragement. It's for leaders who are learning to follow Jesus well. Learning to lead like Jesus is a lifelong education. We never graduate from Christ's leadership school, but we do advance as we become wiser students through our own struggles, failures, and successes.

"Say to wisdom, 'You are my sister,' and call understanding your nearest kin" (Proverbs 7:4 NKJV).

Wise leaders are learners. If they stop learning, they stop leading wisely. Leaders who learn ask the right questions, get the most accurate answers, and make the wisest decisions. How can I get out of the way and support the team to be successful? How can our organization integrate and sustain best practices, to go from good to great? The Lord is eager to pour out wisdom into earnest and humble hearts.

So What Is Wisdom, Anyway?

James, the brother of Jesus, experienced firsthand His wise words and actions. He defined wisdom in this way: "The wisdom from above is first pure [morally and spiritually undefiled], then peace-loving [courteous, considerate], gentle, reasonable [and willing to listen], full of compassion and good fruits. It is unwavering, without [self-righteous] hypocrisy [and self-serving guile]" (James 3:17 AMP). *Learning to Lead Like Jesus* is a distinctly Christian approach from the life and teaching of Jesus Christ. Other traditions have some helpful ideas which I personally respect, but the wisdom of Almighty God cannot be surpassed!

"Jehoshaphat also said to the king of Israel, 'First seek the counsel of the LORD'" (1 Kings 22:5).

Wisdom from Above

Wouldn't it have been wonderfully insightful and inspiring to ask Steve Jobs, before he died, about his greatest creation: the Apple iPhone? Seriously, if we wanted to fully understand this world-changing invention, Steve would be the logical person to ask. What was he thinking? What motivated this design? What was his vision?

In the same way, to understand life and leadership, why not first seek wisdom from the Lord of creation, who made you and me? Doesn't it make sense to learn how to think from the God who molded our minds? Or to learn how to care for our bodies from the one who meshed billions of cells together to make them? Or to learn how to feel and express our emotions from the God who embedded them into our hearts, souls, and spirits? Wisdom from our Maker makes us more like Him. We become like the one whom we love the most.

The Right Use of Knowledge

The prophetic Baptist preacher and prolific writer Charles Spurgeon defined wisdom this way: "Wisdom is the right use of knowledge. To know is not to be wise. Many men know a great deal, and are all the greater fools for it. There is no fool so great a fool as a knowing fool. But to know how to use knowledge is to have wisdom."[1] So my goal in this book is not to present more knowledge that only contributes to making educated fools. Rather, my goal is to rightly present knowledge from Scripture, stories, principles, and instruction about successful habits, to help us become the best we can be in our diverse roles in life.

Not an "11 Easy Steps to Leadership" Book

Learning to Lead Like Jesus is not about simple fixes or avoiding struggles. It's not about how our perfect decisions protect us from all trials and temptations. Rather, it's about 11 character qualities that influence others and will leave a legacy that lasts long after we are gone. These qualities instill the kind of wisdom that allows leaders to make the best decisions under the worst circumstances.

There are many books on leadership today, written by people from a wide array of professions: military commanders, entrepreneurs, journalists, scholars, and ministry leaders. This book is intended to explore that most essential ingredient of leadership: wisdom. What better resource for teaching wise leadership than the Holy Scriptures, the writings that reveal the leadership ways of our heavenly Father, the Holy Spirit, and our Lord Jesus? *Learning to Lead Like Jesus* offers ideas, experiences, guidance, stories, and scriptural references to teach the 11 qualities essential to becoming a wise Christian leader. They are as follows:

Learning to Lead Like Jesus with Humility

In the same way a "gateway drug" is the entry point for other evils, so humility is the starting point for the other ten qualities discussed in these pages. Humility includes preferring others to ourselves and deferring to their needs above our own. With it we can learn and grow for the sake of God's kingdom instead of for the sake of our own little kingdoms.

Learning to Lead Like Jesus with Love

Love is arguably the greatest trait since it is the number one command from Christ. Its attributes, as strung together in Holy Scripture, are compelling:

Love is patient, love is kind. It does not envy, it does not
boast, it is not proud. It does not dishonor others, it is not
self-seeking, it is not easily angered, it keeps no record of
wrongs. Love does not delight in evil but rejoices with
the truth. It always protects, always trusts, always hopes,
always perseveres. Love never fails (1 Corinthians 13:4-8).

Learning to Lead Like Jesus with Accountability

We do better when other people are engaged in our lives. I am part
of a group of four other men called Finishing Well. We meet monthly
to go deep in our conversations, instead of staying on the surface. We
call it scuba diving instead of snorkeling. Our desire is to help each
other see trouble coming and adjust so we can avoid foolish decisions.
Accountability gives others permission to stick their noses into our
business.

Learning to Lead Like Jesus with Relationships

People who allow others to put them on a pedestal, or (even worse)
who place themselves on a pedestal, suffer from pride and are positioned for a fall. It's just a matter of time. However, those who choose
intimacy over isolation are truly rich. Community sets us up to truly
understand others and help them in the best way.

Learning to Lead Like Jesus with Teachability

Sometimes the more knowledge we gain, the less we really know.
When we quit learning we die—maybe not on the outside, but on the
inside our souls shrivel up. Benjamin Franklin stated it well: "Being
ignorant is not so much a shame, as being unwilling to learn." We are
wise to always look around and learn from the people God puts in our
lives. Teachable leaders spend a lifetime learning to lead like Jesus.

Learning to Lead Like Jesus with Discipline

Disciple and *discipline* are similar words. In fact, we cannot become
a disciple of Jesus Christ without some measure of discipline. This is
not about drudgery, but delight. Eric Liddell exercised a rare level of

physical discipline as an Olympic athlete, but an even rarer level of spiritual discipline as a Christian and missionary. This famous quote is from the movie *Chariots of Fire*, about Liddell's spiritual integrity and athletic giftedness: "God made me fast. And when I run, I feel His pleasure." Discipline, motivated by grace, allows us to run our race with holy pleasure over a lifetime.

Learning to Lead Like Jesus with Gratitude

To thank the Lord for the gift of salvation through His Son Jesus is the foundation of gratitude. We should never get over God's amazing grace that saves us from sin, sets us free from sin, and ultimately will deliver us from sin and death. Gratitude draws us close to God. Nothing is more repelling than an ungrateful, murmuring soul, and nothing is more attractive than an attitude of gratitude. We long to linger with thankful souls and hope their joyous attitude will rub off on us!

Learning to Lead Like Jesus with Generosity

I don't recall ever seeing a generous person who was not joyful. Generosity leads to a life that is truly alive. Greed leads to a life that is like Lot's wife, a pillar of corrosive salt, slowly melting into unattractive oblivion. For my new empty nest season of life, my theme verse is Proverbs 11:25, "A generous person will prosper; whoever refreshes others will be refreshed."

Learning to Lead Like Jesus with Forgiveness

Why forgive? Because in Christ, God has forgiven us. We should forgive others for His sake. Forgiveness is freedom: freedom for the forgiver and an opportunity for freedom for the forgiven. Otherwise we only torture our own souls with mind games of revenge, of getting back at our offender. Unresolved anger eats away at our own peace and joy, as well as that of all those in our relational wake. The cross of Christ compels us to forgive others the way He has forgiven us.

Learning to Lead Like Jesus with Encouragement

"How do you know if someone needs encouraging? If they are breathing," said Truett Cathy, the founder of Chick-fil-A. Everyday life steals courage from all of us, so we have the opportunity every day to bring back courage to depleted hearts, and to accept courage from others. Encouragement helps us carry on, knowing we are not alone.

Learning to Lead Like Jesus with Faithfulness

"Well done, good and faithful servant" is the commendation followers of Christ aspire to hear from their Master. Faithfulness is not always fun, but when all is said and done, it is most fulfilling to know we have done our best for our Lord. What does our heavenly Father expect from us? He expects us to do our best, trust Him with the rest, and rest in Him.

I hope you have enjoyed these appetizers from each of the 11 qualities of wise leaders. We will offer broader truths as we move through this book.

How Do We Acquire Wisdom to Lead Like Jesus?

> If any of you lacks wisdom [to guide him through a decision or circumstance], he is to ask of [our benevolent] God, who gives to everyone generously and without rebuke *or* blame, and it will be given to him. But he must ask [for wisdom] in faith, without doubting [God's willingness to help], for the one who doubts is like a billowing surge of the sea that is blown about and tossed by the wind. For such a person ought not to think *or* expect that he will receive anything [at all] from the Lord, *being* a double-minded man, unstable *and* restless in all his ways [in everything he thinks, feels, or decides] (James 1:5-8 AMP).
>
> It is because of him that you are in Christ Jesus, who has become for us wisdom from God—that is, our righteousness, holiness and redemption (1 Corinthians 1:30).

How do we acquire wisdom? The short answer is to ask God, through His Son Jesus Christ. We can be grateful to Jesus for modeling a life that sought wisdom from His heavenly Father. Our Savior escaped into solitude to be with the all-wise One and hear how to move forward by faith. Christ Jesus became wisdom from God for our sake. In Christ we have God's wisdom, and as we learn to love those around us, we grow into wise servants of the Lord. By His grace we are being transformed into wise leaders like Jesus!

Wise Leaders Have Common Qualities

As a cofounder and leader of an entrepreneurial enterprise, and having individually coached, consulted, and trained over 1,000 business and ministry leaders over the past 22 years, I have seen what works and what doesn't in the life of a leader. These 11 qualities characterize those few who are leaders of leaders. By God's grace they embody wisdom in leadership.

In my own experience as a leader, I have been fortunate to serve in safe environments where I was encouraged to take risks and learn from my mistakes. A friend once said to me, "Boyd, as long as you write, lead, and speak out of your weaknesses and struggles, you will never lack content." And boy was he right. This book is based on ideas and lessons from the failures, adversity, and lessons learned by myself and others.

Leading like Jesus is not lived out one way at work, another way at home, and a totally different way at church. Our calling is to lead like Jesus in every context, so people can see consistency as we follow Christ in our attitudes, actions, and conversations. Our faithful lives and humble wisdom brand us as leaders worth following.

None of us are perfect leaders, but in the middle of our imperfections we are honest, vulnerable, and real. Through it all we let go of control and totally trust the Lord. We also trust others and empower them to grow as leaders.

So, what does the Lord require of those aspiring to be a wise leader like Jesus? "He [God] has told you, O man, what is good; and what does the LORD require of you except to be just, and to love [and to diligently practice] kindness (compassion), and to walk humbly with your God [setting aside any overblown sense of importance or self-righteousness]?" (Micah 6:8 AMP).

My prayer is that you will stay in the process of learning to lead like Jesus, and that as you read these stories and ponder the Scriptures, you will wisely integrate these 11 qualities into your leadership.

A student of Jesus,

Boyd Bailey

Roswell, GA

Note: You will greatly benefit from thinking about and acting on the questions at the end of the book!

Chapter One

Learning to Lead Like Jesus with Humility

Don't let selfishness and prideful agendas
take over. Embrace true humility,
and lift your heads to extend love to others.

Philippians 2:3 THE VOICE

Pride makes us artificial, humility makes us real.

Thomas Merton

Jesus Was Humble

Who, being in very nature God, did not consider equality with God something to be used to his own advantage; rather, he made himself nothing by taking the very nature of a servant, being made in human likeness. And being found in appearance as a man, he humbled himself by becoming obedient to death—even death on a cross! (Philippians 2:6-8).

"He humbled himself." The Son of God chose humility so He could serve other human beings. Instead of taking advantage of His divinity for Himself, He emptied Himself for the sake of us. Wow! Humility. Service. Obedience. Death. Salvation. The humility of Jesus is the standard we aspire to as followers of His. J.O.Y. comes from serving Jesus first, Others second, and Yourself third—all with a humble heart.

What Is Humility?

To be humble is to have a healthy view of ourselves, others, and God. C.S. Lewis described humility well:

Do not imagine that if you meet a really humble man he will be what most people call "humble" nowadays: he will not be a sort of greasy, smarmy person, who is always telling you that, of course, he is nobody. Probably all you will think about him is that he seemed a cheerful, intelligent chap who took a real interest in what *you* said to *him*. If you do dislike him it will be because you feel a little envious of anyone who seems to enjoy life so easily. He will not be thinking about humility: he will not be thinking about himself at all.[2]

> **A Point to Ponder:** Humble people leave behind the residue of God, not themselves.

The Problem

Pride and humility cannot coexist. Self-conceit and superiority must be confronted by humility. These two varieties of pride are like prolific vines that choke out all forms of life-giving vegetation. Lewis exposed pride as a major obstacle to knowing God: "As long as you are proud you cannot know God. A proud man is always looking down on things and people: and, of course, as long as you are looking down, you cannot see something that is above you."[3]

The Remedy

Humility is the gateway to grace. "God resists the proud, but gives grace to the humble" (James 4:6 NKJV). Since we are to live the Christian life in the same way we became Christians—by grace through faith—it's imperative we daily infuse our souls with God's grace. If we think we are humble, we are not. But we know the humble Jesus lives in us, with us, and through us. Humility happily defers in love, saying, "How can I honor you above myself?" Wise leaders walk in humility, preferring others above themselves, and deferring to other needy souls.

> **A Point to Ponder:** Humility is the door to walk through to experience God's grace.

Life Lessons Learned over Coffee

"Have the humility to learn from those around you," John Maxwell has said often.

Early in my career I learned about authentic humility from a new friend who was honest and upfront about his thoughts on leadership. Though he didn't specifically use the word *humility* that was what his heartfelt words described.

I was a young pastor in my late twenties. Every day I drove in a modest Nissan 210 into downtown Atlanta to work at a large church, wearing a smart suit, and armed with a desire to serve people. On one of my first days on the job, I sheepishly joined the maintenance team for a hot cup of coffee. They would gather informally to socialize and plan their day. I came to admire one of them in particular, Eddie, for his walk with Christ and his excellent work ethic. He gave me some very wise counsel at the outset of my service at the church.

"Boyd," he said, "most of the 'shirts' [a slang term for the ministers on staff] wait until the last minute to request a room, audio visual equipment, and chairs. There's no problem with one isolated request, but when several leaders forget to give us lead time, then the quality of our service suffers and we feel taken for granted. We are expected to respond to every whim of those who are unprepared. They seem uninterested in me as a person or my success as a co-worker." Then Eddie made a statement that stuck in my heart. "Boyd, what makes me feel respected and valued is when the 'shirts' plan ahead, communicate, and give me proper notice for their room requests so I am able to serve them with energy and excellence."

Eddie's remarks remind me of a military slogan: "Prior planning prevents poor performance."

Wow, what a valuable lesson for a young leader who wanted to serve like Jesus. Here was justifiable frustration from a fellow servant of Christ. He experienced a disconnect between what leaders said about "valuing others above self" and how it played out in the everyday planning of church events.

So, for many mornings over the next six years I arrived early for my cup of coffee and my dose of practical wisdom. I wanted to be a "shirt" who was constantly learning how to better serve those who served with such unselfishness.

> **TAKEAWAY:** *Humble leaders show respect by planning ahead and listening to others.*

A Childlike Trust Asks for Wisdom from a Humble Heart

Let's examine the early career of the wisest man who ever lived, second only to Jesus: Solomon.

> "I am like a little child who doesn't know his way around. And here I am in the midst of your own chosen people, a nation so great and numerous they cannot be counted! Give me an understanding heart so that I can govern your people well and know the difference between right and wrong. For who by himself is able to govern this great people of yours?" The Lord was pleased that Solomon had asked for wisdom (1 Kings 3:7-10 NLT).

Children are so refreshing in their humble and honest questions about God. Over breakfast recently our six-year-old grandson asked me if we will have pancakes in heaven. "Of course," I said. But then I thought, *Wait—is that good theology? Is that really true?* But for my trusting little person, the pancake confirmation opened the door for a string of questions related to what else we will experience in heaven. Humility expresses itself in childlike trust—so simple, and not distracted by adult doubts.

Solomon, the son of David, did not always learn from his father's mistakes, but he did benefit from following his dad's heart for God. With a combination of poetic expression, keen insight, deep understanding, instructive contrasts, everyday examples, and Holy Spirit inspiration, the book of Proverbs provides a baseline of wisdom for any serious student of Scripture.

In the 1 Kings passage quoted above, Solomon reflected on his appointment from the Lord. As the reality of his responsibilities began to weigh on his heart, God, in a dream, asked the new king what he wanted. Solomon humbly replied that he needed wisdom to govern well God's great people, and to know the difference between right and wrong.

Yes! The new leader did not act like he knew what he didn't know. He did not say, "I'll fake it until I make it." Rather, Solomon was real about his lack of experience and knowledge. He knew God's wisdom would allow him to govern well, and he honored the people by recognizing them as the Lord's cherished possession.

How refreshing! What if every government leader, church leader, community leader, business leader, military leader, and family leader approached their task with a humble request for wisdom?

TAKEAWAY: *Humble leaders ask God for wisdom to discern right from wrong.*

A Humble Follower of Jesus Christ Seeks to Educate the Poor

Mother Teresa is one of my favorite followers of Christ. I never met her, but I have met someone much like her. God called Ananthi Jebasingh to start the Good Samaritan School in the late 1980s. A brilliant, middle-aged empty nester with a PhD, she surrendered her life to the Lord in service to the poorest of the poor, never receiving a dime of salary. Her ministry began in her garage in Delhi, India. Barefooted children who begged for food, with matted hair and crusty green noses, hopeful and hungry, filed in like army ants. Ananthi fed their bodies with bread donated by a believer in Christ, and then fed their souls with the Bread of Life, Jesus. The children felt love from this woman who cared enough to open her home and her heart to ragged strangers.

A Point to Ponder: Humility looks for opportunities to teach and serve society's marginalized.

Humility Extends a Legacy for Christ

Ananthi was called by her heavenly Father from the sophisticated halls of higher education to the unsophisticated streets of the slums. When I look at her, I see the face of Jesus. Her quiet humility speaks to me about leadership, wisdom, and obedience.

She learned humility from her earthly father in southern India. Her dad would bring home society's outcasts, the untouchables. Yes, his love for the Lord compelled him to reach out, touch, and love those who otherwise were rejected by their neighbors. The example of her father feeding the homeless, clothing the naked, and giving dignity to the downtrodden lodged deep into her soul. More than anyone I have ever met, she unselfishly honors others above herself.

Now the Good Samaritan School has a main campus and five satellite schools in the slums. Over 1,500 children receive school uniforms, education, nutrition, and minor medical care. Most importantly, they experience love, respect, laughter, security, and salvation in Jesus Christ.

Our family has experienced the joy of having Ananthi as a guest in our home. We hoped our four daughters and our friends might be influenced by her example. Her calling is from heaven, to serve the poor on earth. Ananthi is one of our few living heroes; her humility points us beyond herself and her work to Jesus, to worshipping Him in praise and gratitude.

A Point to Ponder: Humility is built on the example of those who leave a faithful legacy for Christ.

Humility Avoids the Comparison Trap

But wait. Hit the Pause button. Time-out. Isn't Ananthi an icon? Another Mother Teresa? How can we relate to this level of sacrificial love and Christlike commitment? It's a subtle trap for us to compare our calling to Ananthi's. Instead of feeling overwhelmed by her faith and treating her like a super-spiritual saint, we must recognize and embrace our own callings. How is the Lord asking each of us, in our own circumstances, to walk in humility, love, and service to others—especially those without, who suffer in poverty of body, soul, and emotions?

The spiritually bankrupt need our support, as well as those who have lost jobs, homes, or loved ones. All around us are children, teenagers, and adults whom we can love and lead to the Lord with our actions and our words. Ananthi Jebasingh's life is a humble reminder for us to remain faithful to the call to love people different from ourselves. Wisdom in leadership humbly honors others above ourselves. "Do nothing out of selfish ambition or vain conceit. Rather, in humility value others above yourselves, not looking to your own interests but each of you to the interests of the others. In your relationships with one another, have the same mindset as Christ Jesus" (Philippians 2:3-5).

TAKEAWAY: *Humble leaders celebrate the successes of others and are inspired by them.*

Humble Words Heal; Proud Words Hurt

"The tongue has the power of life and death, and those who love it will eat its fruit" (Proverbs 18:21).

Don't you hate it when your words come out too quickly and expose your thoughts too soon? Don't you sometimes wish you could take back your hasty words and have a second chance to not speak so fast? When your tongue gets ahead of your thoughts, the harsh words that come out are from pride, not humility. There is a way to wait before you speak. Let's explore some ideas around how your words can bring sweetness to the soul and healing to the body.

Some leaders motivate by love and encouragement; others by fear and intimidation. I had two different high school football coaches. My least favorite was the intimidator. I feared him because of his tirades and angry, abusive language. I was motivated for a short time, but was afraid I would not do precisely what he wanted. The coach who helped me the most was the encourager. He expected a high standard of performance, but his style was both instructional and inspirational. With him I knew I had room for failure, but my goal was growth.

I saw the first coach as an angry man who expected perfection; he was never totally pleased with me. The second I saw as supportive; he brought out the best in me and expected the best from me. We do our best under leaders who make us feel valued and who challenge us to reach our capacity.

Words matter, and the words of a leader are dissected by followers like a chloroformed frog in a high school biology lab. Wise leaders prayerfully measure their words before speaking.

A Point to Ponder: *Humility offers encouragement that gives life; pride offers discouragement that gives death.*

Our words can get us into trouble or they can dissolve it. Just as a puff of breath can extinguish a candle flame, so a humble word of apology can extinguish the fire of an angry heart. "Please forgive me; I was emotionally spent and did not mean to hurt you with my disrespectful tone." Language brings life when it comes from one immersed in Christ, or death when it comes from one who is indifferent to the Lord. Words matter. When our words come from hearts of worship to God, we are able to bring proper sacrifices of speech to Him.

The power of the tongue must be tamed under the superior power of the Holy Spirit. Otherwise it becomes a weapon of mass destruction. Like radioactive fallout, sinister speech poisons the atmosphere so that what's inhaled into the heart shuts down the spirit. What does it mean to bless others through measured conversations? Water from a hidden irrigation hose snaking through a luscious garden can cause the plants to grow and thrive. So also the language of love gives life by delivering grace to the roots of a thirsty soul.

A Point to Ponder: *Humility allows the Holy Spirit to use words for goodness and glory.*

"Gracious words are a honeycomb, sweet to the soul and healing to the bones" (Proverbs 16:24).

If my heart is full of pride, my words will be laced with a verbal poison of judgment and superiority. If my heart is full of humility, my speech will be seasoned with grace and mercy. If my heart is consumed with fear, I will communicate worry and dread. If my heart is captivated by hope in Christ, I will experience peace and have the courage to speak expectantly of God's faithfulness. If my heart hurts from neglect, I will shamelessly shame another. But if my heart is comforted by the Lord's love, I will have the capacity to give words of comfort. The fruit of healthy words is healing.

"A good man brings good things out of the good stored up in his heart, and an evil man brings evil things out of the evil stored up in his heart. For the mouth speaks what the heart is full of" (Luke 6:45).

Wise leaders are able to empty self and allow Christ to fill their hearts with forgiveness, love, and kindness. God can fill our mouths with fruitful words of encouragement, correction, and compassion. By God's grace we can be Jesus followers whose words bring life to the soul and death to sin! Wise leaders humbly measure their words to bring healing, not hurt, to others.

"Set a guard over my mouth, LORD; keep watch over the door of my lips" (Psalm 141:3).

> **TAKEAWAY:** Humble leaders use words to build up and not tear down.

Humility, Brokenness, Patience, and Persistent Prayer

One of our daughters could not have children. She suffered through years of testing, prodding, probing, and praying. There was anxious anticipation and stress over whether insurance would pay all, pay something, or pay nothing. In the end, the doctor concluded the only hope lay with a special procedure that even then offered only a five percent possibility of pregnancy. Ten days prior to the scheduled procedure our daughter tested again for pregnancy and…it was positive! Amazed and teary-eyed, she administered the home test a second time and remarkably—yes—pregnant! Wife and husband embraced in grateful hope. She called her mom (my wife); her husband called his parents; we all wept together in humble thanksgiving to God. An unfulfilled longing had brought us to our knees, in need of our Father's generous grace—and now, this gift.

Humility keeps us positioned for the Lord's blessings. Our hope may be deferred, but God is still good. Where man gave a five percent chance, the Lord gave 100 percent of His faithfulness, care, and comfort!

"In her deep anguish Hannah prayed to the LORD, weeping bitterly. And she made a vow, saying, 'LORD Almighty, if you will only look on your servant's misery and remember me, and not forget your servant but give her a son, then I will give him to the LORD for all the days of his life, and no razor will ever be used on his head'" (1 Samuel 1:10-11).

Many times humility precedes brokenness. This seems to be Hannah's experience. Unable to have children, she cried out to the Creator—to create within her womb a precious child.

A Point to Ponder: *Humility waits on God's best and resists forcing things to happen.*

Barren. Broken. Rejected. Sorrowful. Ashamed. Just a few of the feelings that could have been in Hannah's hurting heart. Her culture branded her infertility as failure. The inability to have a child was wrongly interpreted by her peers as judgment from God. Brokenhearted but not stewing in self-pity, Hannah humbled herself and called on the name of the Lord to bless her with a son. She vowed with sacred devotion, and pre-dedicated him to the Lord for all the days of his life. Her heavenly Father answered her prayer and blessed her with Samuel, who grew into the godly priest who anointed David, and into whose family lineage Jesus Christ would eventually be born. God blessed Hannah's humility, bold prayer, and desperate trust in Him.

I can't imagine the emotional upheaval of being unable to fulfill the God-given desire for motherhood, to be willing but unable to birth a baby. Perhaps this feeling rivals other unfilled, deep longings of the soul: the longing for marriage felt by a single adult, the yearning for a current marriage to thrive and not just survive, the desire for a work opportunity that seems never to come, or simply the urge to feel known, understood, and loved by another. When our hearts long for someone or something, in our utter brokenness, in our loneliness, our heavenly Father's mercy meets us. His love makes our souls whole. His grace heals our fractured faith.

How's your heart? In humility, have you embraced your brokenness as a pathway to answered prayer, to blessing, to an intense intimacy with God?

> **TAKEAWAY:** Humble leaders use brokenness as a pathway to greater intimacy with God.

Humility Is Willing to Adapt for the Good of Everyone

I can get caught up in my own little world and become oblivious to the needs of my family. Such was the case when we had four teenage daughters at home and I was traveling too much, not realizing the pressure my wife was under. I needed a wake-up call.

In early 2001, I freely traveled around the country leading our national field team for Crown Financial Ministries. Rita, my sweet wife, was at home with our four teenage daughters. One trip was an exhilarating week of serving our leadership teams in California. I had watched Christ bring hope to families who discovered and embraced the Lord's ownership of everything: their calendars, their bank accounts, their stuff, and their relationships. As I returned home, Rita said, "We need to talk." Her tone was serious but hopeful, concerned but caring.

"There are reasons why God's plan is for a dad and mom to parent children together." As she stated the obvious, I began to feel her pain. She continued, "I am glad you are able to travel the world sharing the gospel and loving leaders, but I need more of you at home to help me parent the girls." Rita was so right: boys, homework, boys, volleyball, boys, basketball, boys, church, boys, choir, boys, field trips, boys, drama club, boys, dances, and boys. Did I mention boys?

Small children need their mothers' nurturing, but teenagers can take advantage of their moms. They require their dad's loving firm-ness and patient wisdom to help them manage their growing freedoms.

Sometimes there is no need to pray about the need to do something. I don't need to pray about whether or not to walk across a busy eight-lane interstate, or whether or not to watch the Cubs win the World Series after a 108-year drought, or whether or not to help my wife do what's best for our family. I could trust my colleagues to pick up some of my work responsibilities, but I was the only one who could be the girls' dad. We were able to come up with a simple, easy-to-understand, low-tech plan.

A Point to Ponder: *Humility listens and offers ways to help.*

A red sticker the size of a nickel represented dad being gone one night. After seven stickers were placed on the monthly wall calendar, I would not schedule any additional travel days that month. When a team member would call for me to join them at a leadership retreat, and I explained my calendar already had seven red stickers, no one ever complained. They actually laughed with me at our low-tech solution, and affirmed our accountability system. They then pushed out the request to a later date, or found someone else to stand in the gap, who often did as good a job as I would have—or better.

Rita was delightfully supportive. She could have complained about dad being gone too much. Instead, she gladly explained to the girls, "Guess what? We have dad for 24 days this month. The other seven days, we will pray for him and send him out as a missionary. He can help people grow in their relationship with the Lord, and can encour-age them to faithfully serve others."

What seemed like a career disruption actually allowed our family to grow closer with each other and closer to Christ. By hitting the Pause button and adjusting, we prepared for future leadership opportunities that required a strong and stable family unit, with the necessary emo-tional energy and spiritual stamina.

When we do what's best for the family, or for the team, or for the organization, and then trust God with the outcome, He steps in and grows healthy relationships and strong organizations. Humble leaders look for what's best for the family or the business, not just what's best for personal gain. They replace selfish ambition with godly ambition.

TAKEAWAY: *Humble leaders do what's best for "us," not just what's best for "me."*

Humility Shares the Credit and Takes the Blame

"By the grace given me I say to every one of you: Do not think of yourself more highly than you ought, but rather think of yourself with sober judgment, in accordance with the faith God has distributed to each of you. For just as each of us has one body with many members, and these members do not all have the same function, so in Christ we, though many, form one body, and each member belongs to all the others" (Romans 12:3-5).

If things go wrong, my natural tendency is to "give reasons" or even blame another. But if things are successful, I enjoy taking the credit and can forget to celebrate with the team and my family. I can fail to recognize the contributions of everyone in the positive outcome. It's harder to take the blame and share the credit. I experienced this first-hand with a colleague at work.

I once worked with a colleague who felt the need to receive credit for any team project he participated in. At first it was annoying. Not fair. I and the other three team members, whose contributions were equally as important, felt the injustice. One night over dinner I complained about this. My wife, Rita, said, "Sounds like he has a deep desire for significance that needs to be filled." I didn't want to hear words of compassion. I wanted justice, and for him to grow up! But over time I learned she was right. He gained confidence and began to outgrow hoarding the limelight. We all learned to give each other credit for success.

If any one person holds on to credit for success, it corrupts. It corrupts judgment by leading them to think more highly of themselves than they should. Wise leaders quickly give away credit to others and to the team as a whole. Credit given recognizes the contribution, skill, and smarts of all the staff.

A humble leader knows that sharing credit goes together with delegating well. Stellar execution and follow-up can't occur unless associates give tedious attention to details and implementation. Secure leaders can't wait to give away the credit. Like a wad of cash burning a hole in your pocket, it burns a hole in the ego. Wisdom in leadership understands how to value others and their unique contributions to the organization. As Harry Truman is known to have said, "It is amazing what you can accomplish if you do not care who gets the credit."

Wisdom in leadership also takes the blame for failures, and shows how we should take responsibility for our actions. Wise leaders keep the buck of blame instead of passing it along. They are as quick to take the blame as they are to share the credit. Like a surge protector, they keep the team from suffering an undeserved shock of failure. Mature leaders stand in the gap. They have no claim to fame, but they do take the blame when things go wrong.

A humble leader's example of blame-taking is infectious to followers. Followers unconsciously find themselves emulating the same blame ownership in their spheres of influence. "I am responsible," or "It's my fault" are common statements of blame-takers. When you learn how to effectively take blame for failures and give credit for successes, you exhibit wisdom in leadership. Faithful leaders trust the Lord, who in turn blesses them. The Holy Spirit empowers people through wise leaders who share the credit and take the blame.

TAKEAWAY: *Humble leaders give credit for successes to others and to the team.*

So what comes to mind about the level of humility in your own leadership? Maybe there are one or two ideas you can apply to grow your humble heart. Before you set your next goal, consider helping another meet their objective. Or when you are at a restaurant, make it about the server's needs, not about the server meeting your every need. Pay attention, listen, and you will learn better ways to help those around you. Most of all reflect on the life of Jesus and humble yourself like He humbled Himself: willingly and obediently!

Summary of Chapter One Takeaways

1. Humble leaders show respect by planning ahead and listening to others.

2. Humble leaders ask God for wisdom to discern right from wrong.

3. Humble leaders celebrate the successes of others and are inspired by them.

4. Humble leaders use words to build up and not tear down.

5. Humble leaders use brokenness as a pathway to greater intimacy with God.

6. Humble leaders do what's best for "us," not just what's best for "me."

7. Humble leaders give credit for successes to others and to the team.

Chapter Two

Learning to Lead Like Jesus with Love

Serve one another humbly in love.

Galatians 5:13

The first job of leadership is to love people.
Leadership without love is manipulation.[4]

Rick Warren

Jesus Was Loving

"Greater love has no one than this: to lay down one's life for one's friends" (John 15:13).

Jesus was love and He modeled love. He extended compassionate love to sinners who were aware of their sin but unaware of God's forgiveness. He also dished out tough love to the religious establishment who were unaware of their sin but expecting God's approval. Christ's love was holistic. He fed and healed bodies, and He healed the brokenhearted by forgiving their sin and teaching them how to follow Him.

A Loving Leader Emphasizes God's Love

"The source of love that motivates loving leadership is God's unending, unconditional love for us"[5] (Glenn C. Stewart).

My grandmother always had a way of encouraging me, but also challenging me to become better. One such occasion was in my junior year in college. I had just given what I thought was a pretty good sermon at the evening church service. She greeted me with the smile of a proud grandparent, hugged my neck, left a smudge of beige makeup on my collar, and said, "Son, that was a good sermon, but you need to talk more about God's love. You can't talk too much about the Lord's love." Now at 57, I'm still trying to talk more about the Lord's love. She was so right. All these years of experiencing the Lord's lavish love have motivated me and empowered me to love others well.

"We know and rely on the love God has for us. God is love. Whoever lives in love lives in God, and God in them" (1 John 4:16).

We are called by Christ to love with a love not of this world. It is a love that can only be explained by an encounter with Almighty God. His transforming power positions His disciple to love on His behalf. The parting words of our Savior presented a new, radical love language for His disciples: "As I have loved you, so you must love one another" (John 13:34). Jesus's command is the best motivation for leaders to love well! So, show God's love by helping others, and spread God's love by speaking to others in the name of Jesus.

> **A Point to Ponder:** We are loved by the Lord to love for the Lord.

Loving Leaders Are Influenced by Loving Leaders

Yes, our Lord and Savior Jesus Christ is our best example of how to love, but what about others in our lives who love well that we can learn from? Early in our marriage we met one of those unusually loving couples.

In seminary (graduate theological school), my friend Jim asked if I was interested in some extra work after classes—mowing a lawn, planting flowers, gardening, and bush hogging (cutting brush). This would be on the farm of his boss and mentor, Mr. Sammons. Offering extra income to a seminarian was like dropping red meat in front of a hungry, skinny dog. I said, "Yes! Let me talk with Rita." I was sure she would be delighted for us to have some discretionary cash for date night, baby clothes for our two-year-old, or to buy a cute outfit without feeling guilty. As for me, I was always in need (or want!) of another cool book to devour. Expectantly, I soon met Mr. Sammons at church.

The first impression I had of my future boss and mentor was of a joyful, gentle, and engaging man. His wife, Fay, looked at him with tenderness, favor, and love. Only a few years before, their marriage was a train wreck because of Jim's affair with his work. He learned the hard way that his infatuation with success and money had become a mistress. His neglect almost drove away the one he admired the most—his wife. I related to Mr. Sammons since he was a broken man who recognized he would walk with loving dependence on the Lord for the rest of his life.

Mr. Sammons's example showed me how proud, successful leaders can build walls around their hearts, shunning others. But when leaders admit their failures, weaknesses, and struggles, they can build bridges to other hearts because they are real and relatable.

A Point to Ponder: Love's openness builds bridges to other brokenhearted people.

I felt shy and insecure around wealthy people. Growing up with my single-parent mom and two brothers in my grandmother's 800-square-foot, wood-framed rental property, we were intimidated by those who lived in the brick homes in Country Club Estates. Government-issued cheese, powdered milk, and food stamps were necessary to keep our modest expenses from exceeding our little income. I did not relate well to the rich.

I sheepishly saw myself as a "yard man," but Mr. Sammons called me his "landscaper." Wow. That sounded like someone smart, useful, and valuable. I was not an isolated, anonymous "yard man," but his personal, professional "landscaper." He respected me as an individual, and he and his wife, Fay, honored my family by getting to know us in such a way they could pray for us with understanding.

A Point to Ponder: Love prays for individuals with knowledge and understanding about them.

I had been a Christian for only two years when we arrived at seminary. Yes, I was ignorance on fire! I had more energy than sense. In a burst of enthusiasm, naively but sincerely, I told Rita, "Sweetie, Billy

Graham is getting up there in age and someone needs to step up and take the baton to preach the gospel in stadiums around the world." We dreamed of packing six future children into a recreational vehicle, homeschooling, and crisscrossing the country while I shared the good news of Jesus to packed-out evangelistic crusades. Gratefully, my ambitious ignorance was directed down a more productive path by my fellow traveler in the faith.

Routinely on my work break Mr. Sammons taught me the Scriptures. I told my mentor of my self-appointed succession plan for Billy Graham. Instead of bursting into laughter, Mr. Sammons very gently and lovingly pointed me back to a biblical example. "Boyd, when I look at the life of Paul, his pattern was to follow the Holy Spirit's leading to a certain population of people, put down roots, share the gospel, disciple new Christians, and encourage the church." Mr. Sammons helped me connect my good intentions to the reality around me. Instead of aspiring to be an itinerant evangelist, I needed to establish my work in a community and grow my influence for Christ.

> **TAKEAWAY:** *Loving leaders show kindness to others by treating them with honor and dignity.*

Loving Leaders Learn Patience

"Love is patient" (1 Corinthians 13:4).

Patience has a calming effect on everyone under its influence. Impatience does just the opposite. A person huffs and puffs until everyone knows he's unhappy for not getting his way. Thankfully, love lengthens the fuse of patience. Love builds capacity to care about what another person might be experiencing. Love looks behind the angry face to see the hurting heart, and then shows mercy to the person, who may be crying out for help.

A few years ago, a business owner told me the following, with an attitude almost like a badge of honor: "Boyd, I am not a very patient leader at work. When things are not going well, my short fuse causes me to blow up, yell at everyone, and get them back on track. I know this is probably not the best approach, but it gets the job done." After seeing my friend's chaotic work culture and the carousel of staff coming and going, I came to agree with him. Impatient anger is not the best approach!

Are your circumstances trying your patience? Has someone gotten on your last nerve and exhausted your patience? If so, join the crowd of those of us who need a fresh perspective of God's patient love. Yes, while we were still sinners, the Lord patiently allowed His Son Jesus to suffer, so we could be set free from the shackles of sin. Christ loves us patiently, to the point of bearing our burdens. We are not discarded, but loved, in spite of our inconsistencies.

"God demonstrates his own love for us in this: While we were still sinners, Christ died for us" (Romans 5:8).

A Point to Ponder: Loving patience responds with a cool head and resists a hotheaded reaction.

By God's grace we demonstrate patient love toward those who do not demonstrate patient love toward us. Our frustrated friends could be stuck in their own crazy cycles of sin, still in need of a Savior. They are not capable of loving patiently because they have yet to receive the genuine love of their heavenly Father. Those of us who commune with the Prince of Peace know better. Those who lack peace also struggle with patience. Love is patient with impatience.

See your marriage as a laboratory where you can learn how to patiently love another. Take the high ground of grace when you are hurt. Explain to your husband or wife, with loving patience, the pain you feel you carry alone. Let them in on your fears, dreams, and angry feelings. When you express your emotions with patient love, you give permission for your spouse to do the same. Your love may be stretched for a season, but your patience will reflect God's grace.

"Jesus looked at him and loved him" (Mark 10:21).

Heavenly Father, thank You for loving me patiently,
so I can love others patiently.

TAKEAWAY: *Loving leaders are long-suffering in their love for the unlovely as well as for the lovable.*

Loving Parents Cool Down and Learn Not to React Harshly

Parenting is not for the faint of heart. Exhaustion makes it harder to hold back a sarcastic remark that can bruise the heart of a precious child. I am much more spiritual when I'm rested! I've done my share of going back to one of our daughters to ask for forgiveness. Fortunately, as I grew older I learned what not to do.

On more than one occasion I have had emotionally elevated conversations with our daughters—especially when they were teenagers. Sometimes I became angry and, with a harsh, demanding tone, said, "You are wrong and you will do what I say!" Because of my impatient desire to fix things and move on, I failed to really listen and know my teenage daughter. Eventually I realized how boneheaded my approach was.

Many times, with concern, my sweet wife, Rita, would call me out. "Boyd, you were too rough. You need to apologize." She would be right, so I would go back and apologize to my little girl, and ask her to forgive me for reacting out of anger instead of with gentleness and understanding. I was in a crazy cycle of anger and apology, of demanding respect and compliance and then regretting how I did it. Then I discovered a better approach. I have implemented this at work, with friends, and at home.

When the tone of my voice begins to rise, when my throat dries out, and my palms are sweaty, I call a time-out. I say something like, "Let's take a break, cool down, and get a good night's rest. Then in 24 hours we will reconvene and pick up our discussion with a calmer tone." When we take the time to follow this cooling-down technique, we come back with a greater willingness to understand the other and work together toward a solution. Anger is an unhealthy state from which to speak our minds. Loving leadership waits for a better day. Wisdom in leadership would rather protect the relationship than win the argument.

Poetry provides a refreshing way to see life and engage our hearts from a different perspective. Below is a poem about love by a gifted writer, George Herbert (Anglican priest 1593–1633), followed by an explanation of the poem by much more of a scholar than I.

Love

LOVE bade me welcome; yet my soul drew back,
    Guilty of dust and sin.
But quick-eyed Love, observing me grow slack
    From my first entrance in,
Drew nearer to me, sweetly questioning
    If I lack'd anything.

"A guest," I answer'd, "worthy to be here":
    Love said, "You shall be he."
"I, the unkind, ungrateful? Ah, my dear,
    I cannot look on Thee."
Love took my hand and smiling did reply,
    "Who made the eyes but I?"

"Truth, Lord; but I have marr'd them: let my shame
    Go where it doth deserve."
"And know you not," says Love, "Who bore the blame?"
    "My dear, then I will serve."
"You must sit down," says Love, "and taste my meat."
    So I did sit and eat.

George Herbert's "Love" has one basic meaning and one deeper meaning…the basic meaning is the poet on a romantic dinner with a lover. The deeper meaning is that the poet is a lost soul that God is helping. The Lord tells the poet to "sit down…and taste my meat," inviting him to eat his flesh and drink his blood. The poet accepts God's power as well as his own faults, "So I did sit and eat." This last line again refers to Communion, as the poet takes God into himself. In this act he accepts God's forgiveness and shows respect to God's sacrifice on the cross for all sins, taking all blame. Love (God) is at the door and our main character is declaring his unworthiness in joining love. He specifically says he is not worthy to look upon love. But Love says that it is fine because "Love made his eyes."[6]

Love accepts others as they are. Probably all of us want to love more and love better. But it is easy to get consumed with our own life issues. It is also easy, as the poem states, to not feel worthy to be loved by God. But only if we accept God's love for us can we love others. Gratefully, Jesus has a way of cutting though our cluttered hearts and making things clear.

What Is Your Capacity for Love?

"Therefore I tell you, her sins, which are many, are forgiven—for she loved much. But he who is forgiven little, loves little" (Luke 7:47 ESV).

One of our family members has been deeply hurt in life. Broken relationships, broken marriages, broken finances, and broken health. Unfortunately, brokenness has evolved into bitterness in his heart. According to him, everyone else is at fault. Sadly, he sits in his pity party alone. No one else attends. My heart aches for this loved one who feels trapped and destined to a miserable life of unforgiveness. Because he can't receive much love, he can't give much love. Only love received can be breathed back out into another life.

The measure of our forgiveness forms the depth of our love. A person who is forgiven much loves much. Outside of God's grace, we all have the same wall of sin between Christ and ourselves. We are separated from God by our sins, but the cross of Christ tore down sin's barrier. By faith, we are forgiven of our sins and adopted by God as His children. By receiving the grace of God we transition from the rags of this world to the riches of heaven.

Forgiveness is cause for gratitude and thanksgiving. For some, forgiveness seems greater because the sin is greater. Or, upon further reflection, maybe our sin debt was more serious than we were willing to admit. Maybe the lust in our hearts was addictive. Maybe the anger in our attitude was caustic. But God forgave us, and He still forgives us. This is another reason for love to resonate in our hearts. Not only has Christ forgiven us of past sins, His grace also cancels out present and future debts of sin. Such is the massive depth of His forgiveness.

> **A Point to Ponder:** My capacity to love is based on my experience of God's great forgiveness.

You can love much because you have been forgiven much. Gratitude explodes from your heart when you ponder the depth of His forgiveness. All sin—past, present, and future—is wiped clean. The guilt is gone. The shame is erased. Your conscience is clear. You are freed from sin to love. Your gratitude toward God compels you to love Him and others. Sin has been replaced with your Savior, Jesus. He loves through you. Love is your primary language because you have been changed. You are a new creation in Christ. It takes a little getting used to because of the sinful habits attached to your past life, but you are a new person.

Christ became your life. Now you live from the inside out. Your heart is full of love and forgiveness because of what God has done for you. You love continually and passionately because He loves you with an everlasting love. Meditate on and measure the extent of your forgiveness from God. Can you fathom where you would be without the grace and forgiveness of God? Celebrate His forgiveness with love. Thank Him often for His forgiveness. Show your appreciation to God for His forgiveness by loving others unconditionally. Love the undeserving. He did; He does; and He will. The forgiveness of God is matchless, boundless, and freeing. It facilitates love and produces love. Let this truth consume and compel you. To be forgiven is to love. You can love much because you have been forgiven much.

"We love because he first loved us" (1 John 4:19).

From whom do I need to ask forgiveness, and whom do I need to forgive so my capacity to love can expand?

> **TAKEAWAY:** *Loving leaders grow the capacity to love when they experience forgiveness often.*

Loving Leaders Are Motivated to Obey Christ

Most of us want to understand the "bottom line" when we are in relationships—the basic thing that is really going on. Is the bottom line that he wants me to do something? Is the bottom line that I just lost my job and am seeking sympathy? Is the bottom line that she doesn't want to keep dating, and wants me to understand why? Jesus stated very clearly the bottom line proof of our love for Him: obedience. "If you love me [Jesus], keep my commands" (John 14:15).

To be motivated by love is foundational to the Christian life. So, we must honestly ask, what motivates our faith and good deeds? Is it love for Christ?

> Do we serve because we love?
>
> Do we worship because we love?
>
> Do we pray because we love?
>
> Do we give because we love?
>
> Do we work because we love?
>
> Do we share the gospel because we love?
>
> Do we make disciples because we love?

Wisdom in leadership is motivated by love.

Love is foundational to obedience, and obedience is the outcome of love. Love for God leads to obeying God. Christ's commands are instructional to a loving heart. As our hearts are harnessed together with His, we are yoked together in His love (Matthew 11:28-30). We learn to value what He values. For example, we see Jesus ministered to someone of a different race, to a habitual sinner, and to someone from a different social status. So we too seek to minister to all people, even those very different from us. Love is expressed by obedience to Jesus!

"Jesus replied, 'Anyone who loves me will obey my teaching. My Father will love them, and we will come to them and make our home with them'" (John 14:23).

> **A Point to Ponder:** *Obedience to God is evidence of our love for God.*

Loving obedience is not cold and calculated, but rather warm and Spirit led. It is not just checking a box on Sunday church attendance or dutifully caring for needy souls throughout the week. Discipline can rigidly uphold a moralistic code of conduct for a time. But true obedience to Jesus is when His love flows through our lives, giving life to others. Christ empowers us to love on His behalf. He is love! Words of love without follow-through are spurious. Our test of love is our obedience.

How do we answer Jesus when He asks us, as He asked Peter, "Do you love Me? Do you really love Me? Do you really, really love Me?" (see John 21:15-19).

We can only say "Yes" to Jesus's question if the fruit of love is evident in our lives. Forgiveness, kindness, compassion, patience, and humility all mark a disciple of Jesus. Love does the hard thing when it is especially hard to do. Love loves the unlovely. Love looks intently into the life of Jesus and seeks to love like He loved. We enjoy our heavenly Father's love so others can enjoy His love in us. Love motivates us to trust, love, and obey!

"In fact, this is love for God: to keep his commands. And his commands are not burdensome" (1 John 5:3).

Heavenly Father, fill me with Your love so I
am able to love others like You love.

> **TAKEAWAY:** *Loving leaders are motivated to love by obeying Christ's commands.*

Loving Leaders Never Give Up

It is not easy to keep showing up and not give up, especially when we have already lost, failed, or been embarrassed. Are you kidding me? Am I really supposed to go through that pain again, or at the very least, the fear of being rejected again? Maybe you need to be willing. Sports is one of those arenas where you can't hide—you either keep going or quit.

Please allow me to use an example from college football. Thank you, and since I've been an Alabama fan for 57 years, I am relying on God's grace to explain this objectively. Ha!

Dabo Swinney is a proven winner on and off the football field. A reporter asked him this question just after Clemson's 2017 National Championship win over Alabama: "Dabo, you've been in this game before, but how would you describe what it's like to win it?" His answer:

> It's indescribable. I mean, you can't make it up, man. I mean, this is…only God can do this—take a guy like me from Pelham, go down to Alabama, win a national championship, come to Clemson and then have a chance to win a national championship against the best team in the country up until the last second of this game. And to see my guys fight, just believe. I told them tonight, I told them that the difference in the game was going to be love. It's been my word. My word all year has been love. And I said, "Tonight we're going to win it because we love each other. We are going to love each other. I don't know how we're going to win it." I told them at the halftime, "Guys, we are going to win the game. I don't know how, but we're going to win it." And man, just, I'm just so thankful and blessed. It just doesn't even seem real to me.

Love is what motivated Dabo and, probably with a similar intensity, his coaches and players. Dabo is a loving leader. He leads with love. He loves the Lord, he loves his family, he loves his team, and he loves people in general.

I met Dabo at a Chick-fil-A Bowl prayer breakfast a few years ago and mistakenly thought he was Shane Williams with the Fellowship of Christian Athletes (FCA). They look like twins! Dabo was so gracious with my social mishap, he went along with my friendliness by asking if I had met his wife, Kim. I shook Kim's hand, thanked both of them for all they were doing to support FCA, and shared about when I was a senior in high school and FCA dramatically moved my heart closer to Christ.

Dabo even loves people like me who confuse him with someone else. True confession: I may be as big a Dabo fan as I am a 'Bama fan. Don't tell my father-in-law; he might cancel my fan card!

> **TAKEAWAY:** *Loving leaders persevere when motivated by the greater purpose of love.*

Loving Leaders Have a Healthy Love of Themselves

"Love your neighbor as yourself" (Matthew 22:39).

Why do we beat ourselves up so badly? Sometimes I feel we set a harder standard for ourselves than what the Lord expects from us. Guilt. Fear. Shame. These lying whispers are not what define us. We are to love ourselves because God loves us. The object of His love matters. We matter more than all the rest of His creation, plus He commands us to love ourselves. So how? Here's a love plan.

Self-love sounds narcissistic. It can be, but the self-love the Bible teaches results in selflessness. Dignity and respect for ourselves develops dignity and respect for others. A healthy love of ourselves contributes to a healthy love of others. Lack of self-love results in self-loathing, even self-disgust. We are emotionally stunted and struggle to receive outside love if we cannot accept and love ourselves. Our Creator loves us unconditionally, so we can also. Here are four ways we can love Him, others, and ourselves well: soul care, emotional care, physical care, and care for others.

1. Soul Care

We care best for our souls by first experiencing our souls' salvation in Jesus Christ. Only a saved soul is capable of loving itself in a healthy manner. Through prayer we are able to receive the comfort and affection of the Holy Spirit. When we are filled with the Spirit we are full of love. Yes, we feed our souls when we study and apply God's Word. His truth reminds us of our 100-percent acceptance in Christ. We feel loved when we see ourselves as the Lord sees us. A cared-for soul seeks Jesus, avoids sin, and loves the Lord, others, and itself well.

"We love because he [God] first loved us" (1 John 4:19).

2. Emotional Care

What does it mean to care for our emotions? First, we receive Christ's care. He forgives our sins. He heals our broken hearts. He comforts us in our sadness. He holds us securely. Second, we process our feelings in a way that helps us understand how God made us. We may have a need for approval, so we learn to seek it from God instead of people. Emotionally we have limitations, so we learn our limits and then trust the Lord to meet unmet needs. Emotional care learns to pace itself in prayer. Hope, faith, gratitude, and community contribute to loving ourselves well.

"Above all else, guard your heart, for everything you do flows from it" (Proverbs 4:23).

3. Physical Care

The Holy Spirit is a resident of our bodies. Are we attentive landlords for our special tenant? How do we take care of our bodies? A healthy intake of food and drink is responsible physical management. Sleep deprivation and lack of exercise is not. Since we cherish the Spirit's presence, we care for our bodies. Since we are the hands and feet of Jesus, we aspire to good health, so we can help others. Love nourishes the body. As Paul explained, loving our bodies is on par with loving our wives: "In this same way, husbands ought to love their wives as their own bodies. He who loves his wife loves himself" (Ephesians 5:28).

4. Care for Others

How well we can love others is determined by how well we can love ourselves. We are able to love our neighbors well when we love ourselves well. For example, if we attend a meaningful marriage retreat, love compels us to share what we learned and thus bless others, or perhaps even sponsor another couple to attend a future retreat like the one we experienced. If we are blessed to enjoy fulfilling work, love compels us to help the unemployed find work. Wisdom in leadership is selfless in its love for others.

"Let no debt remain outstanding, except the continuing debt to love one another, for whoever loves others has fulfilled the law" (Romans 13:8).

*Heavenly Father, lead me by Your Spirit to
love myself and others as You love.*

TAKEAWAY: Loving leaders are able to love others well when they love themselves well.

Loving Leaders Are Already Successful

"Love never fails" (1 Corinthians 13:8).

What a relief to know we don't have to strive hard for many years, or obtain some level of immense net worth, to be successful. God has one success factor: LOVE. When we love well, we are successful, and when we do not love well, we have failed. Wow, a pass or fail test on how to live an abundant life for the Lord!

There is a 100-percent guarantee: When love is applied, it will succeed. For instance, love finds a person stuck in their sins and woos them back into a loving relationship with the Lord and their loved ones. Love finds a way to work things out when a disagreement erupts over conflicting opinions. Yes, love by nature is set up for success; it is always reliable. Love is the default behavior for Jesus followers. Wise leaders measure success by how well they love others.

We give life to others when we die to ourselves. So, in marriage we seek to out-serve each other. We value our spouse's needs above our own. Our selfless love brings out the best in our mates. Yes, we migrate from wanting to have it our way to finding satisfaction in seeing it their way. Successful marriages are built on selfless love. We are blessed when we choose to first bless our best friend.

"Truly, truly, I say to you, unless a grain of wheat falls into the earth and dies, it remains alone; but if it dies, it bears much fruit. Whoever loves his life loses it, and whoever hates his life in this world will keep it for eternal life. If anyone serves me, he must follow me; and where I am, there will my servant be also. If anyone serves me, the Father will honor him" (John 12:24-26 ESV).

> **A Point to Ponder:** The language of love naturally flows from the lips of loving leaders.

Is your leadership language laced with love? Are your actions accompanied by love? If so, you are a raging success in God's eyes. Look for ways to love, and you will never lack opportunities. Be a successful lover of the Lord and people, and you will be energized by the joy of obedience to God's greatest commands. Every day you love is a day you succeed for your Savior. Today, in Jesus's name, love every human being you meet, at their point of need. Why? Because God gave His only Son for them (John 3:16).

The Lord's love doesn't fail for one second. You may feel like a failure, but His love lifts you up to live another day for Him. Your circumstances will not consume you, because Christ's love is your protection. Like a fire-retardant blanket, the love of God shields you from the fiery flames of fear. If you run away, His love does not stay away. When you make mistakes, His mercies are new every morning. You succeed when you receive the love of your heavenly Father!

"Because of the LORD's great love we are not consumed, for his compassions never fail" (Lamentations 3:22).

Heavenly Father, thank You for loving me so I can be a leader who loves well on Your behalf.

> **TAKEAWAY:** Loving leaders are successful when they are loved by the Lord and love others well.

So love is a great backdrop for being a wise leader like Jesus. Humility is the easel, love is the canvas, and Jesus is the artist! Ask yourself and the Lord, "What's one thing I can do today to love better?" Do the same thing tomorrow, and you will be a loving leader!

Summary of Chapter Two Takeaways

1. Loving leaders show kindness to others by treating them with honor and dignity.

2. Loving leaders are long-suffering in their love for the unlovely as well as for the lovable.

3. Loving leaders patiently look for a better way and wait to speak on another day.

4. Loving leaders grow the capacity to love when they experience forgiveness often.

5. Loving leaders are motivated to love by obeying Christ's commands.

6. Loving leaders persevere when motivated by the greater purpose of love.

7. Loving leaders are able to love others well when they love themselves well.

8. Loving leaders are successful when they are loved by the Lord and love others well.

Chapter Three

Learning to Lead Like Jesus with Accountability

Each of us will give an account of ourselves to God.

Romans 14:12

It is not only what we do,
but also what we do not do,
for which we are accountable.

Molière

Jesus Was Accountable

He withdrew about a stone's throw beyond them, knelt down and prayed, 'Father, if you are willing, take this cup from me; yet not my will, but yours be done.' An angel from heaven appeared to him and strengthened him" (Luke 22:41-43).

Jesus was accountable to His heavenly Father. Under the pressure and pain of His humanity, He asked for another way, knowing His Father's way was the only way. What a freeing thought, to know we can ask for a way out, but still accept God's will as the best way. The cup of the cross did not pass, but an angel of the Lord did pass by to strengthen Jesus to carry out God's will. Accountability to His heavenly Father's will was what mattered most to Christ, and it should be the same for all who follow Him. In prayer God bends our will to His will in obedience to His greater good.

What Is Accountability?

When we give others permission to stick their noses into our business, to ask the hard questions, and to call us out when our behavior does not match what we say we believe, we are accountable. Trusted friends who love us should love us enough to question our motives and move us closer to the heart of Christ. The person whose spouse feels comfortable to call a friend of theirs to share a concern about their behavior—that is accountability. The goal is not just to keep us from foolish decisions, but to grow us in wise decision-making. Good questions help us examine our hearts.

Twelve accountability questions that can clarify our intentions:

1. Why do you want to…(change your job, leave your church, go into debt, etc.)?

2. How does the Bible address this issue?

3. What does your spouse think?

4. What's best for your family, your faith, and your friends?

5. Does this decision align with your life purpose and long-term goals?

6. Are there any of your actions or attitudes you would not want posted on social media?

7. Are you sure you want to do this?

8. Have you adequately prayed about this decision and thought through its implications?

9. Are you reacting out of anger and fear, or responding out of forgiveness and faith?

10. What advice would you give someone else in your situation?

11. Is this the story you want to write for your life and later have told about you?

12. What would Jesus do?

In the Christian community, accountability, like prayer, is talked about more than it is practiced. Why? One reason is we lack a plan and process to implement either of them. Someone asked me as a young man to prayerfully consider writing out a "Life Plan." As I began to write down the desired outcomes of my life, I realized that putting my plan on paper set me up for accountability. It brought clarity and substantially increased my motivation to follow through.

Surround yourself with those who will tell you the truth in love. Find objective friends whose desire is for you to follow God's will for your life. Accountability is the Lord's instrument to protect you from yourself and from the penalty of poor decision-making. We all make mistakes, but accountability minimizes them. The wise leader gladly submits to accountability.

"The king answered the people harshly. Rejecting the advice given him by the elders, he followed the [unwise] advice of the young men" (1 Kings 12:13-14).

> **TAKEAWAY:** *Accountable leaders take the time to develop plans and work them.*

Accountable Leaders Are Cautious

I like to look at the lives of men and women who finish well and follow their example. "Remember your leaders, who spoke the word of God to you. Consider the outcome of their way of life and imitate their faith" (Hebrews 13:7). I met Dr. Billy Graham in Atlanta at one of his crusades before the Olympics. He was bigger than life and is still one of my heroes. Years ago I read a biography of him. Many stories about his wise and faithful life inspired and intrigued me, but one in particular gave me pause and immediately altered my life.

Dr. Graham never traveled alone. At least one associate always accompanied him, and he would not meet privately with a woman other than his wife. I once heard it said, adultery does not start in the bed, but over coffee, alone with another woman. After preaching to a packed-out stadium, an exhausted Dr. Graham went back to his hotel, but before he entered his room a team member opened the door and discovered a woman wearing nothing but a raincoat. Her plan was to place Billy in a compromising situation. Fortunately, his friend whisked the woman out before any damage could be done—avoiding the appearance of evil.

Adultery is impossible if a man is never alone with a woman who is not his wife, or if a woman is never alone with a man who is not her husband. Old fashioned? Probably. Too narrow? Perhaps. Wise? Absolutely. Is there a better question than, "Is it right or wrong?" Maybe we should ask, "What is the wise thing to do?" Prepare now, by setting a plan before a sticky situation arises. For instance, driving two separate cars to the same meeting may be necessary to not risk the appearance of impropriety between you and a colleague of the opposite sex.

> **A Point to Ponder:** Accountable leaders are cautious, not cavalier, about the appearance of wrongdoing.

Unaccountable Leaders Are Flippant About Foolish Choices

In Atlanta a few years ago, the male founder of a major ministry made the mistake of giving a female associate a ride to the airport, with just the two of them in the car. Innocent enough? Not really. A few days later, she accused him of inappropriate personal behavior. Since they were alone, it was her word against his; no one else was around to witness what really happened. After months of "he said/she said," the ministry board ask him to step down as president.

A lifetime of good work ended with humiliation over a one-hour drive alone with another woman. A colleague of the once-respected leader made this sad observation after the 70-year-old founder was fired by his ministry's board of directors: "I don't know if any of the allegations, then or now, are true. They were never proven. But [he] certainly made some bad judgments. It's hard to believe he'd get in a car alone with a female member of the staff, even after so many years. He put himself in a situation in which he has a hard time defending himself."

Wise leaders construct guardrails around their lives to protect themselves from skidding off the slippery slope of a foolish decision.

> **TAKEAWAY:** Accountable leaders avoid compromising situations by having clearly defined boundaries.

Accountable Leaders Fear God and Submit to Authority

"If you do warn the righteous person not to sin and they do not sin, they will surely live because they took warning, and you will have saved yourself" (Ezekiel 3:21).

Fear of God tends to be ignored or looked down on as a passé belief, only for old-school fundamentalists. If so, Jesus fit the category. He said, "I will show you whom you should fear: Fear him who, after your body has been killed, has authority to throw you into hell. Yes, I tell you, fear him" (Luke 12:5). The love of God without the fear of God is not genuine, only man-made and artificial. Fear of God causes us to run toward moral authority and run away from sin.

Let's see how an accountable leader can gain the high ground of moral authority by fearing God.

Recently, I met with my "Finishing Well" accountability group of five guys for a cookout. Our host is in the food service industry, so the meal was fabulous. The conversation was even meatier. After dinner, our discussion focused on one friend who was stung by a recent string of harsh statements from his wife. He vented by giving specifics and asking for advice. All of us probed with more clarifying questions and discovered he had not talked to his wife about her critical comments. One of the guys suggested the hurt husband talk with his spouse on how they might improve their marriage. Such a simple idea, but it gave perspective and permission to address the issue.

Effective accountability groups are engaged and involved, not passive. Once someone invites a friend into their life for accountability, it is a serious responsibility. Accountability is active, engaging, and encouraging. The giver and receiver of accountability enter into a trusting relationship. Wisdom in leadership listens to the warning of an accountability partner or group.

Wise leaders give permission to a few friends to hold them accountable. A bit of short-term discomfort and embarrassment can save a lot of long-term regret. When you encounter emotional situations, keep a level head. Accountability facilitates objectivity. When you are under pressure, call on the help of an objective team that can give you wise perspective. Your accountability group is there as a buffer against unwise decision-making.

A Point to Ponder: Authentic accountability requires caring confrontation.

"Better a poor but wise youth than an old but foolish king who no longer knows how to heed a warning" (Ecclesiastes 4:13).

Hard decisions can paralyze us into inaction. Accountability provides much-needed courage for us to do the right thing. Avoiding a difficult decision today will compound its inevitable consequences in the future. Accountability encourages us to not procrastinate when we are afraid. It relieves our fears and bolsters our faith.

For example, a team member may need to be reassigned, for the good of the organization and for their own good as well. A prospective church volunteer may need to be told "no" because they are not ready for a leadership role. Your young adult children may not be prepared for marriage because they need to first move away from home and experience independent living. Accountability helps facilitate God's will. Wise leaders are able to give or receive an answer of "no" now, trusting that a better "yes" will come later.

Above all else, live like you are accountable to Almighty God, as one day we will all give an account to Him for our actions.

"They are surprised that you do not join them in their reckless, wild living, and they heap abuse on you. But they will have to give account to him who is ready to judge the living and the dead" (1 Peter 4:4-5).

Am I truly accountable to God and others, and do I provide effective accountability to friends?

TAKEAWAY: *Accountable leaders fear God, submit to authority, and invite accountability.*

A Community of Loving Accountability

Christian leaders are not meant to lead alone, but with others empowered by the Holy Spirit. A loving community provides the best accountability because there is nowhere to hide. We all do better where we are known and where we know others. Acceptance in a safe environment is designed to keep us from sin and foolish decisions while emboldening us with the faith and courage to passionately follow Christ.

A couple of years ago I asked four men my age to join me in a ten-year commitment to a "Finishing Well" group for accountability. They are all admired leaders in the Christian community with a lot of autonomy, a lot of family and career success, and years of earning a good name. All was at risk without wise and loving accountability from true friends. Some of us were already friends and some were acquaintances. But we all needed a safe environment to go relationally deeper, to not just "snorkel" with surface conversations, but "scuba dive" deep into the dark waters of trials and temptations. We meet monthly for two hours over lunch at one friend's office in Atlanta. In addition, together we attended a men's conference with transformative teaching, and were able to engage one another's hearts at a deeper level. We have kept our relationship real and rewarding.

I experienced a similar group of guys when I was younger. Some groups are seasonal—they run their course. It might be a year-long Bible study, a book club, a mentor group, a Sunday school class, or a home small group. Consider a combination of environments to remain accountable. Wisdom in leadership prayerfully looks for friends who model and inspire accountability.

TAKEAWAY: Accountable leaders do better because others are watching what they do.

Wise parents provide loving accountability for their dating-age children. Rita and I challenged our four girls as they approached their dating years to consider these ideas as a beginning filter for marriage:

1. Marry your best friend.
2. Make sure your heart flutters.

3.   Make sure they love the Lord more than they love you.

When our girls turned 13, Rita and I made a big deal about them becoming teenage young ladies. Thankfully, Rita had already done the awkward "birds and bees" talk with them. Now my role was to describe to our sweet girls how precious they were to me, to their mom, and most importantly, to their heavenly Father. I explained how we would pray with them for the special man to come into their life who would be their best friend, make their heart flutter, and love the Lord more than he loved them. We prayed for husbands they could do ministry with—not mates who would become lifelong ministries!

I planned for the daddy/daughter date to feel special and memorable for each of my little girls. I dressed up in a suit, and my beautiful, youthful, innocent date wore her Sunday best. She could pick any restaurant in Atlanta for our dreamy time together. Three daughters chose steak houses and one chose Asian cuisine—I didn't complain! Prayerfully, enthusiastically, and intentionally, we scripted together a life story they could enthusiastically tell their child one day.

A Point to Ponder: Is the life story you are writing what you want to tell your future family?

Prior to each special dinner, Rita ordered a unique gift for me to present—a classy but godly reminder of our daughter's desire to save herself for a special man in marriage. The necklace contained a heart with an embedded lock in the middle, and a dangling key. As her dad, I would securely keep this symbolic key to her heart until the Lord sent into her life His man just for her. In the meantime, I dated each daughter individually, and by God's grace attempted to model how a man is to express courtesy, respect, and love in a healthy relationship.

We arrived at the restaurant with the necklace hidden in my sport coat. Inside the small gift-wrapped package was a personalized poem I had written, with verbal images illustrating each daughter's personal uniqueness and temperament. I wanted them to feel known and deeply valued by their dad. Before the meal was served, I excused myself to the restroom, found our server, and gave him the small package to bring out on a silver tray at the end of the meal.

Once the lid on the sparkling tray was lifted, all of our emotions elevated to new heights of giddy expectation. Tears flowed from tender eyes and my proud heart as she read the poem customized to show her how much I cared about what she cared about. Wisdom in leadership provides creative and loving accountability for their children.

> **TAKEAWAY:** *Accountable leaders clarify for their families what's most important in life.*

Wise parents provide loving accountability for those dating their child. Rita shared with me her God-given intuition when one of our girls began to get emotionally involved and physically attracted to a particular young man. Our job was difficult, since not one of our four daughters were ugly, but stunningly beautiful like their mom. And these teenaged boys were everywhere, clawing to get into the door of our home and into the girls' hearts!

Soon after my wife would share her concern, I would invite the hormone-heavy young stud for a man-to-man talk at the Waffle House, a Southern-style diner with tasty grits and fresh coffee. After exchanging pleasantries about the weather and sports, I would ask a pointed question to address the 800-pound gorilla in the room: "What is your plan to stay pure with my daughter?" One young man said he was not comfortable discussing this topic with me. I said, "Wrong answer," and proceeded to ask if he had a prepared game plan for the college football games he played. Wasn't there a much higher probability of success when he had a plan and followed it?

After choking down his last bite of waffle, he decided to move on from our daughter and date someone else. We were not heartbroken! But the four men who married our girls all thanked me for asking them the hard questions and for holding them accountable. One even said, "Mr. Boyd, thank you for asking. No man has ever held me accountable to stay pure, not even my own dad." Once they drafted their purity plan supported by Scripture, I asked them to invite two mentor couples to hold them accountable to follow the plan!

> **A Point to Ponder:** *Are you available and emotionally engaged in the lives of your children?*

Wise Parents Pray for Their Child to Meet the Lord's Choice for a Lifetime Mate

Several years after our oldest daughter, Rebekah, graduated from Auburn (though an Alabama fan, I was an Auburn investor for four years!), she met a special young man while working in DC. Todd was from Atlanta and came highly recommended from a mutual friend of ours. The family joke was that Rebekah's high standard for a husband was a combination of (1) Jesus, (2) Tom Cruise, and (3) her dad, so it might take years for her to tie the knot. Known as "brother Todd," they started out as friends, but soon grew a more serious relationship.

Serendipitously, they both attended a DC gathering with Truett Cathy for words of wisdom and encouragement. Todd, who has never been accused of being shy, approached Truett after his talk, with Rebekah in hand, and asked for his best business advice. The Chick-fil-A icon did not miss a beat. "Marry the right person!" Wow. "Yes," I thought when Todd and Rebekah related their conversation to Rita and me, "marry someone who loves what you love, who will dream with you, and who will give you the confidence and emotional support to be successful!" Timely advice for the couple who would soon marry.

Wise Parents Ask Their Adult Children to Write a Pre-Marriage Accountability Plan

For our readers I have a bonus, like the extra footage from a good film. My daughter and son-in-law, Rebekah and Todd, gave me permission to share their plan to stay pure before marriage and wait for their special day. Below is the first half of their plan. You can access the second half specifics at www.wisdomhunters.com by using a key word search with Todd and Rebekah.

Biblical Foundation

Colossians 3:1-17

- Christ commands for our sinful self to be put to death, "Put to death therefore, whatever belongs to the earthly nature: sexual immorality, impurity, lust, evil desires and greed" (Colossians 3:5).

- Once we surrender and allow Christ to put to death the old self, we are to be consumed by the new self Christ has for us, "Put on the new self, which is being renewed in knowledge and in the image of its Creator" (Colossians 3:10).

- This new self is a life characterized by "compassion, kindness, humility, gentleness and patience. Bear with each other and forgive whatever grievances you may have against one another" (Colossians 3:12-13).

Ultimately our mind should be so consumed with Christ that it naturally filters out what is not honoring to Him.

1 Corinthians 6:12-20

"Do you not know that your body is the temple of the Holy Spirit, who is in you, whom you have received from God? You are not your own: you were bought at a price. Therefore honor God with your body" (1 Corinthians 6:19-20).

Our bodies are the temple of God. They are special and bought with the ultimate act of love—the death of Christ. We are to honor Him by preserving what He died for (our sins) by abstaining from sexual immorality.

Philippians 4:8

"Whatever is true, whatever is noble, whatever is right, whatever is pure, whatever is lovely, whatever is admirable—if anything is excellent or praiseworthy—think about such things" (Philippians 4:8).

We are called to be consumed by the thoughts of Christ and they are to dictate our lives. Inevitably a life characterized by these traits will lead to a life of peace.

Mission

Our mission is to glorify God in everything we do. We seek to specifically honor and glorify Him in relating to each other throughout the process of our relationship.

Purpose

Our purpose is to strive to serve and honor each other while seeking God's best for the relationship. Throughout this process we will continue to grow to a deeper level with each other.

Strategy

Our strategy is to honor and protect each other's whole person (emotions and body) while seeking God's best for our lives.

Tactics

See the tactical elements of Todd and Rebekah's purity plan at www .wisdomhunters.com.

We agree to the above written document:

Signed: Todd Coons   Signed: Rebekah Bailey

TAKEAWAY: *Accountable leaders have purity plans, and mentors who hold them to their plans.*

Wise Parents Celebrate the Engaged Couple's Faithfulness on Their Wedding Day

Fast-forward to each daughter's wedding. I quickly embraced the role of the father of the bride:

1. Sit down…be patient!
2. Shut up…be quiet!

3. Shell out…be generous!

> **A Point to Ponder:** *We learned after the first wedding to set a budget, give them the cash, and let the newlyweds keep what they didn't spend.*

I had the joy of officiating at all the weddings of our four daughters. At the outset of the first ceremony another minister asked, "Who gives this bride?" Emotionally I replied, "Her mother and I, and her three sisters." Pause. Remember my little 13-year-old and the "key" to her heart I kept until she met God's special man for her? Well, I pulled it from my pocket, slipped it into the hand of the groom, and whispered, "Don't screw up!" OK, I didn't actually say that last part, but it did cross my mind.

After giving my daughter's hand in marriage to my soon-to-be son-in-law, I stood in front of friends and family to officiate their wedding. And yes, I did recount the dinner date at age 13, and the handoff of the "key" just moments before. We all wept and celebrated Christ's faithfulness. And by God's grace I was able to make it through the surreal experience of the ceremony and declare, "You may kiss the bride!" We experienced versions of that first wedding three more times over 11 years. Each location was in turn less formal—first a red-brick, white-column city church; then a rustic, wood-beam country church; then an open-air barn; and finally a cotton warehouse—but each venue in turn cost more. Ha!

Wisdom in leadership invests in the present for the desired outcomes in the future.

> **A Point to Ponder:** *Do the right thing now and trust the Lord for the right outcomes later.*

Wise Parents Provide Loving Accountability After Their Child's Wedding

Another example of living in accountability comes from our

relationship with our four sons-in-law. Twelve years ago I learned from a friend the idea of a monthly one-hour conference call, to stay connected and to encourage and challenge all five of us at once. This was not easy when one son-in-law was in graduate school in Cape Town, South Africa, and another was in Vancouver, British Columbia, attending seminary. Because of the nine-hour time difference, noon on Saturday worked best for all. I explained to the guys our time was an investor's call. We all have a lot invested and we need to evaluate our return on investment!

We came up with three questions for each of us to discuss on our call:

1. What is the Lord teaching you?
2. What are you learning from your family?
3. What is your biggest challenge at work we can pray about for you?

Most of the time our calls are not made up of neat, 12-minute segments for each of us. We allow additional time for someone who may have an extra challenge he is facing. He may need more time for wisdom, encouragement, or correction. Rita and the girls talk every day, but guys need the reminder of a date on the calendar to make sure we are engaged in each other's lives.

A Point to Ponder: *An agreed-upon process can facilitate robust and real relationships.*

A few years ago the sons-in-law and I traveled to Buena Vista, Colorado, for four days in July. The wives were gracious to hold down the forts while we played on four-wheelers across the Continental Divide, swam in a chilly mountain lake, sledded down a snowy peak, and ate delicious meals. On the last day of our adventure we gathered on the back deck of our cabin and looked out on a vista of fourteeners (mountains exceeding 14,000 feet). The view was breathtaking.

As we gazed on God's creation, I challenged the guys to take their

Bibles and their journals and each enjoy a 30-minute prayer walk while pondering, "Lord, how do You want me to serve my family during this season of my life?" On cue they arrived back on the deck for our debrief. Each one's temperament was evident in their prayer walk reflections. Todd, the oldest, is a Georgia Tech Yellow Jacket, so his thoughts were neatly organized on his computer. Tripp, an Anglican priest, recorded his quiet reflections in a rugged leather journal, written with monastic-type calligraphy. J.T., an engaging sales guy, had his etched in his brain, not yet put to pen and paper. Tyler was not with us yet, but no doubt with his contemplative temperament he would have written down on his phone or journal some prayerful thoughts to consider.

Each one, vulnerable and transparent, discussed topics like the need to travel less and be home more, to serve as a patient dad and loving husband. One was considering a job change. Another had just changed careers and was seeking opportunities to make his mark in the new role. Our conversation was rich and real. Our trust and respect for each other grew exponentially. Like kudzu in a warm, moist climate, accountability thrives in a safe environment full of trust, love, and respect. Wisdom in leadership schedules fun times seasoned with serious moments.

TAKEAWAY: *Accountable leaders engage with communities of accountability.*

Accountable Leaders Set Deadlines to Drive Decisions

"Elijah said, 'As the LORD Almighty lives, whom I serve, I will surely present myself to Ahab today.' So Obadiah went to meet Ahab and told him, and Ahab went to meet Elijah" (1 Kings 18:15-16).

We have all been with groups that have lots of ideas but very little follow-through. After a while people become unhappy about the unproductive hours and begin to not take the meetings seriously, sometimes avoiding them altogether. Hopefully none of us have to endure any more of these time wasters. Here is an idea to use simple deadlines and move projects forward to completion.

In our work at Ministry Ventures we learned to set specific and attainable deadlines to drive decision-making. Deadlines provide a sense of urgency and accountability internally for our team, and externally for the ministry leaders we serve. For example, an opportunity to receive a scholarship may only be valid for 30 days and limited to the first ten organizations who sign up for our online certification. Deadlines facilitate action. I am much more focused when I have a writing or project deadline. Firm deadlines, set by prayer, drive me to make better decisions for God.

Elijah, a prophet of God, felt compelled to call out the false prophets of his day. He asked his friend Obadiah to set up a meeting with King Ahab, who was the authority over the prophets of Baal. Obadiah convened the two strong wills for a testy meeting. The king charged Elijah with being a troublemaker, which he denied. The prophet then accused the king of deserting Yahweh. He challenged Ahab to use his influence to immediately call out the pagan leaders. The king brought together 850 false prophets, and Elijah brought with him the one, true, living God Almighty. A prayerful, bold deadline unleashed the dramatic power of God's glory.

"'Answer me, LORD, answer me, so these people will know that you, LORD, are God, and that you are turning their hearts back again.' Then the fire of the LORD fell and burned up the sacrifice, the wood, the stones and the soil, and also licked up the water in the trench. When all the people saw this, they fell prostrate and cried, 'The LORD—he is God! The LORD—he is God'" (1 Kings 18:37-39).

A Point to Ponder: *Tension and conflict often require a bold and clear challenge.*

Procrastination could delay a blessing the Lord Jesus has for your life. Low priority tasks may be more fun and easier, but high priority tasks bring the best long-term fulfillment. Schoolwork can be tedious and onerous, but deadlines along the way move your education forward. Incremental growth of understanding is much better than last-minute memorization with little comprehension. If you put off today what you can do tomorrow, you may miss a God opportunity. Be faithful with a small, unpleasant task today and trust the Lord for a larger, pleasant possibility tomorrow.

See deadlines as the Spirit's way to show you the best way. What would you do differently if you only had one year left to live? Take those ideas that come to mind and prioritize them around helpful deadlines. Short deadlines can keep tasks simple, while long, drawn-out deadlines may bring too much complexity. Focus on one problem at a time, and do not be overwhelmed by a dozen things at once. Also, be flexible when a faith opportunity arises. Deadlines drive decisions, but be willing to adjust based on the Spirit's leading. Be decisive, act, and trust God. Wisdom in leadership is courageous to set deadlines and trust Christ with the process and with the outcomes.

"He did this so that all the peoples of the earth might know that the hand of the Lord is powerful and so that you might always fear the Lord your God" (Joshua 4:24).

Heavenly Father, give me the focus to set prayerful deadlines so I am a better steward.

TAKEAWAY: *Accountable leaders set deadlines to help facilitate healthy decision making.*

Accountable Leaders Learn to Say No

Our "noes" should define us more than our "yeses," otherwise we are merely reacting to everyone else's whims, agendas, and crises. Jesus did not respond to every request. Even when His good friend Lazarus was dying, the Lord said "no" so God could be glorified with something greater—resurrection! So, by faith, wise leaders become accountable to themselves to say "no" or "not yet." When you say "no" as a leader, you can save room for a better "yes!"

As a young man working in churches driven by hyper-programming, I learned the hard way how to say "no!" I very much needed to feel the approval of the church members I served. Whether it was someone sick in the hospital, or a new Christian who wanted to meet for early morning prayer and Bible study, or a couple seeking premarital counseling, I said "yes"—99.9 percent of the time.

Officiate weddings? Yes! Direct funerals? Yes! Drive a bus to pick up children from the housing projects? Yes! Monday night visitation? Yes! Wednesday night prayer meeting? Yes! High school summer camp counselor, which included a 2:00 am search for three senior boys who somehow escaped out an unsecured window and were nowhere to be found? Yes! And then there was the winter retreat when one of our 16-year-old girls was missing at 11:00 pm. Later she wandered back and sheepishly explained she was only on a prayer walk. Really?

Rita reminds me that being available for people is part of my calling from God. That's a very good reminder, but where I lose perspective is when my motivation gets hijacked by drivenness. My unhealthy need for approval keeps me on a frantic pace that is unsustainable and unwise. I am too often driven by the flesh to please people, instead of being led by the Spirit to serve. Sometimes my fears and insecurities mislead me, but when I passed age 40, I learned a new, helpful word: "no!"

> **A Point to Ponder:** *It's better to take the risk of disappointing people who don't know you than to routinely disappoint those close to you.*

Out of my fatigue and frustration, it began to dawn on me: If I aspired to be Super Christian, I would eventually burn out. Just as important, I would hinder other well-meaning followers of Jesus from using their gifts and abilities to serve people. In other words, with my all-consuming service I wasn't allowing other, more qualified leaders the opportunity to step up and be blessed. Jesus said, "It is more blessed to give" (Acts 20:35). I needed to spread the love around and allow other giving hearts to enjoy the fulfillment of loving people. I began to learn a hard lesson: A need does not necessarily require me. I can trust someone else—who many times is better equipped and has a higher capacity to serve.

If I try to do everything for everyone, I risk not doing anything well for anyone. The reality is I only do a few things extremely well, and those gifted differently than me complement my skills. A leader is not called to be a one-man band, but rather a skilled orchestra conductor/composer—like Leonard Bernstein (of the New York Philharmonic), who made sure everyone had finely tuned instruments, and all played with precision and harmony and from the same sheet of music. Wisdom in leadership orchestrates the beautiful music of unity within diversity!

> **TAKEAWAY:** Accountable leaders are defined more by their "noes" than their "yeses."

Wise Leaders Train and Trust Others, While Inspecting What Is Expected

When leaders become accountable to not try to do everything themselves, they are freed up to do what they do best, and to empower others to do what they do best. I have been there. When I was younger I had more energy than sense, and I could do everything. Or so I thought—until I came to realize that I was spread too thin, had no emotional energy for my family, and was trying to live in perfection. And, of course, perfection is not possible in this life, so my work suffered. But the Bible gives us great insight in how to slay this spirit of trying to do everything.

Many times it's more expedient to do the work ourselves. It goes faster, with fewer mistakes, and there's not the headache of training someone. However, doing everything ourselves is not the most effective leadership approach in the long run, as we quickly max out our capacity. Emotionally, overextended. Mentally, no margin. Physically, exhausted. Spiritually, spent! Wisdom in leadership learns to train up other faithful leaders.

"The things which you have heard from me in the presence of many witnesses, entrust these to faithful men who will be able to teach others also" (2 Timothy 2:2 NASB).

Moses woke up one day and discovered all decisions were flowing through him. Though it stroked his ego, he was on the verge of not doing anything well because he was trying to do everything himself. Fortunately, someone he really respected (his father-in-law, Jethro) spoke into his life:

"Moses' father-in-law replied, 'What you are doing is not good. You and these people who come to you will only wear yourselves out. The work is too heavy for you; you cannot handle it alone'" (Exodus 18:17-18).

Not only was Moses on the precipice of physical, emotional, mental, and spiritual collapse, so were those seeking his advice—all of them were about to "wear [themselves] out" (verse 18). Reality can be a harsh teacher. It's better to anticipate the need to surround ourselves with a diversity of gifted leaders than to wait until after the fact and find ourselves causing unintended strife and stress.

A Point to Ponder: Accountable leaders listen to and act on good advice.

Jethro's advice was clear and simple: Instruct and show the people how to live and resolve their own issues in accordance with the Lord's ways. When they are unable to agree on a solution, involve an objective third party to mediate and help them come to a resolution.

> Listen now to me [Jethro] and I will give you [Moses] some advice, and may God be with you. You must be the people's representative before God and bring their disputes to him. Teach them his decrees and instructions, and show them the way they are to live and how they are to behave. But select capable men from all the people— men who fear God, trustworthy men who hate dishonest gain—and appoint them as officials over thousands, hundreds, fifties and tens. Have them serve as judges for the people at all times, but have them bring every difficult case to you; the simple cases they can decide themselves.

That will make your load lighter, because they will share it with you. If you do this and God so commands, you will be able to stand the strain, and all these people will go home satisfied (Exodus 18:19-23).

Moses took the time to prayerfully recruit capable, faithful men of integrity and wisdom. They were trustworthy and feared God. He gave them a specific scope of work and set a clearly defined number of people under them, for these leaders to help in settling disputes. As a result, the people went home satisfied, and Moses was able to handle the strain of his responsibilities. Wisdom in leadership looks for ways to delegate to capable leaders.

As a father-in-law to four sons-in-law, my favorite verse is, "Moses listened to his father-in-law and did everything he said" (Exodus 18:24). Yes!

> **TAKEAWAY:** *Accountable leaders take the time to follow up and inspect what's expected.*

Accountability sounds hard, and it can be, but in the long run it is freeing. Cars can travel faster, safer, and farther around curvy roads when there are secure guardrails. In the same way, we can travel through life as significant and successful leaders if we submit to accountability from God above and accountability from family and friends below. Today ask four other people to join you in intentional, loving accountability!

Summary of Chapter Three Takeaways

1. Accountable leaders take the time to develop plans and work them.
2. Accountable leaders avoid compromising situations by having clearly defined boundaries.
3. Accountable leaders fear God, submit to authority, and invite accountability.

4. Accountable leaders do better because others are watching what they do.

5. Accountable leaders clarify for their families what's most important in life.

6. Accountable leaders have purity plans, and mentors who hold them to their plans.

7. Accountable leaders engage with communities of accountability.

8. Accountable leaders set deadlines to help facilitate healthy decision-making.

9. Accountable leaders are defined more by their "noes" than their "yeses."

10. Accountable leaders take the time to follow up and inspect what's expected.

Chapter Four

Learning to Lead Like Jesus
with Relationships

*Walk with the wise and become wise,
for a companion of fools suffers harm.*

Proverbs 13:20

Shared joy is a double joy; shared sorrow is half a sorrow.

Swedish Proverb

Jesus Was Relational

While Jesus was having dinner at Matthew's house, many tax collectors and sinners came and ate with Him and His disciples. When the Pharisees saw this, they asked His disciples, 'Why does your teacher eat with tax collectors and sinners?'" (Matthew 9:10-11).

Jesus was relational because He loved people, especially people who claimed no religious devotion. He took His disciples with Him to the house of Matthew, a despised man, frowned on by his fellow Jews for being a Roman tax surrogate. Jesus knew the best way to get to know someone was to be with them where they lived. He invited His followers to join Him so they could learn how to better love sinners. Christ was criticized by the religious elite for being too familiar with sinners, but our Lord was happily fulfilling His mission "to seek and to save the lost" (Luke 19:10).

A Homeschooling Mom Who Values Relationships over Results

Rita and I have a very good friend who sets a good example in serving as a homeschooling mom and a genuinely supportive wife, as well as a wise friend. We admire how, even with her zeal for structure and results, she keeps the number one priority on growing relationships—her relationship with the children, and their relationships with each other.

It was a typical morning in the Randolph house as Aria assembled her four children in the living room for their first lesson of the day. She invited the kids to start off with a song. After the first few notes, a fight erupted between her two oldest sons, Kenyon and Isaac. Soon, harsh words were exchanged, and Kenyon ran upstairs.

Aria was tempted to leave Kenyon alone while she continued to focus on the other children so the outburst wouldn't derail their daily schedule. But then she remembered one of the guiding principles that she and her husband, Josh, had adopted for their family: putting relationships first.

As she headed upstairs to collect her son, she thought to herself, *What good is it if I teach a great lesson this morning but my kids are at odds with one another and our house is divided?* She decided to not go any further until the relationship between the brothers was restored. As a humble leader of her family, Aria's approach is to put relationships first. Wisdom in leadership prioritizes relationships first.

"Command them to do good, to be rich in good deeds, and to be generous and willing to share. In this way they will lay up treasure for themselves as a firm foundation for the coming age, so that they may take hold of the life that is truly life" (1 Timothy 6:18-19).

Aria explains, "When my kids are 30, I want them to be able to have healthy relationships. That means knowing and being known by God, and knowing and being known by the people He puts in their lives. I know too many people who did well on the SAT exam but don't know how to steward the relationships in their life well. I want more for my kids than a good college education and a nice paycheck. I want to lead them into a life that is truly rich in relationship with God and others."

> **A Point to Ponder:** *Rich relationships with God and people are the truest riches to be enjoyed.*

To lead her children well, Aria believes that spending time reading and memorizing God's Word is vital to her personal growth. She also emphasizes that staying connected through community and mentors is important. "I go to church and we have a fantastic Sunday school class with six other mentor couples. I also have one-on-one time with a mentor on a regular basis, and I'm part of an amazing small group that continually challenges me."

Perhaps one of the most important principles Aria and Josh have learned is leadership by example. One way they model the importance of relationships to their kids is by making certain they don't neglect one another. They make their marriage a priority by being intentional with their time together through daily check-ins in the evening, regular date nights every week, monthly business meetings to discuss the family budget and calendar, and several yearly vacations as a couple. By putting one another first, they are showing their children the best way to treat their future spouses. As parents they are on the same page with how to love and lead their family.

So how do wise leaders measure success? Aria still believes traditional measurements have their place. She says, "I measure some of my success by how my kids are doing academically. We test according to state standards, and I breathe a sigh of relief every time I get back scores that say I'm doing my job well. But that's kind of the bare minimum."

True success for Aria as a homeschooling mom shows up in different, unexpected ways. "I consider it success when I see my boys wrestling together on the couch like best friends," she says. "Success is when I see them choose to serve others without being asked, or when they choose humility and confession when they're in the wrong, or when they work outside the home and get hired back again because they have a great work ethic. And certainly, success is when I hear my teenager say, 'Thank you!'"

"The job of leading my children is far from finished," Aria says. "Every day I'm reminded of the wise counsel of some of my older friends who keep telling me I can't measure it all now! I will keep my eyes on Jesus and continue to lead by being intentional with my time and putting my relationship with the Lord and my family first."

TAKEAWAY: *Relational leaders value relationships—sometimes more than measured results.*

The Quality of Our Lives Is Influenced by the Quality of Our Relationships

"Walk with the wise and become wise, for a companion of fools suffers harm" (Proverbs 13:20).

You probably desire quality relationships, but are you willing to pay the price of investing in others with the goal of providing more value than you receive?

What does it mean to have quality of life? Is it good health? Harmony at home? A happy heart? Financial security? Freedom of speech and worship? A fulfilling career? Grateful and contented children? A meaningful marriage? A life of significance? Peace with God? Probably some of these elements and more make up a life worth living, a quality life.

Relationships matter because the quality of our lives is influenced so heavily by the quality of our relationships. Who we spend time with is who we become. If we spend time with those who are wise with their finances, we too can become wise with our finances—if we pay attention. If we worship with those of great faith, we too can grow in our faith. Our lives reflect our relationships.

"Therefore I urge you to imitate me. For this reason I have sent to you Timothy, my son whom I love, who is faithful in the Lord. He will remind you of my way of life in Christ Jesus, which agrees with what I teach everywhere in every church" (1 Corinthians 4:16-17).

So how is your relational portfolio? Is it diversified with people who bring value to all aspects of your life? Conversely, are you intentional in investing time and interest in those who look to you for guidance? Quality of life flows not just from receiving wisdom but from giving wisdom. Wisdom works both directions for the good of relationships.

A Point to Ponder: Our relational investments are our greatest assets.

Be careful not to excuse bad behavior because you are trying to relate to questionable company. Draw a line, and stay far away from eroding your character. You don't have to join in the bad to be an influence for the good. In some situations, what you choose not to do defines you more than what you choose to do. Use business trips and vacations to model faithfulness, not foolishness. Stand for what's right when others bow to what's wrong.

"Do not be misled: 'Bad company corrupts good character'" (1 Corinthians 15:33).

Above all, quality of life results from your relationship with Christ. He is life itself, and everything good in life flows from Him. When you grow in your personal relationship with Jesus, it affects the growth of all your other relationships. Relationship building with heaven builds relationships on earth. Ultimately, Jesus's life is the one to follow and model. The resurrected life of Christ gives you the spiritual stamina to experience a quality life.

"Jesus said to her, 'I am the resurrection and the life. The one who believes in me will live, even though they die; and whoever lives by believing in me will never die. Do you believe this?' 'Yes, Lord,' she replied, 'I believe'" (John 11:25-27).

Who are the wise people I spend time with? Am I investing in quality relationships?

TAKEAWAY: *Relational leaders understand how relationships affect their quality of life.*

A Relational Lover Like No Other

I've known Dan Glaze many years. I was first attracted to his warm smile and keen, listening ears—he uses them both! Trained as an engineer at Georgia Tech, he is a relational enigma. He will tell you it has taken him a long time to develop his skills to love people well.

At work we all affectionately refer to him as the "Mayor" of National Christian Foundation (NCF). Dan knows how to love on people and invest in them. This is his calling at NCF, where he's a

National Relationship Manager. Rita and I love and admire Dan and his wife, Donna. Wise leaders are always growing and increasing their relational investments and love for people!

Below are three questions I asked Dan regarding relational investments, followed by his answers.

1. What does it mean to invest in others relationally?

    Investing in others relationally is sharing life upon life. Today's culture is driving us toward isolation. We are spending more time looking at our phones than being face-to-face with people. I am confident that life cannot exist outside the context of relationships. We have limited time and energy, and the most important use of our time is to invest in the lives of others. Investing in others relationally means laying aside our desires for self and giving our lives to someone else. By the way—this is what Jesus did!

2. Why do you invest in others relationally?

    There is a saying that only two things will last eternally: God's Word and people. What then is worthy of our investment? Transformation (life change) takes place in relationships, not in isolation. I desire to be God's touch into people's lives. There is nothing more important than sharing life together. People are lonely today because they are building walls instead of bridges.

    But the main reason I invest in others is because this was God's strategy for bringing life to a dead world. Emmanuel (God with us) selected *purposeful proximity* as His strategy. He could have come as an idea or a light, but He came as one of us and walked with us. The word *relationship* comes from the Latin *relationem* meaning "a bringing back, restoring." So many of us have the tendency to get off track from being who God desires us to be. Relationships bring us back and restore us to who God created us to be, with intimate relationships with Jesus Christ.

A Point to Ponder: To have meaningful relationships requires a prayerful process of investing our time.

3. How do you invest in others relationally?

I pour my life into the lives of others. I care for them. I invest in others by being more concerned with their needs than my own needs. I take a keen interest in their lives, their relationships with Christ, their families, their businesses, and their hobbies. There is one couple Donna and I met back in 1994. That year Donna and I intentionally decided to invest in this couple's lives. What an amazing journey over the last 13 years! Each year we spend four days together at their lake house laughing, eating, praying, crying, fishing, and loving each other. Chuck and Joanne have become almost as close as family.

As I seek to serve and give to others, I end up receiving far more than I give. God's economy is upside down from today's culture. As I invest in the lives of others, God gives a huge return into my life. There is no greater ministry than investing in others.

Anthony D'Angelo states, "Treasure your relationships, not your possessions." Relationships will give a greater return.

"A new command I give you: Love one another. As I have loved you, so you must love one another. By this everyone will know that you are my disciples, if you love one another" (John 13:34-35).

TAKEAWAY: *Relational leaders value the eternal significance of relationships.*

Relational Investment Plan

"To Titus, my true son in our common faith: Grace and peace from God the Father and Christ Jesus our Savior" (Titus 1:4).

Some people have systematic plans to invest money over long

periods of time so there is a compounding effect. Why not take the same approach by investing in relationships? Paul gave us a live example of how he intentionally took on Timothy, a protégé worth a lifetime investment of time, energy, and money. He did for one what he wanted to do for many.

Relational investments compound into eternity. Yes, loving people takes time, effort, and perseverance, but the dividends pay off handsomely. For example, we can regularly read a children's Bible to our little one and not see immediate character change, but hopefully over time they will accept the Scriptures as God's wisdom and love letter to them personally. The best fruit from family faith investments is when our son or daughter embraces faith in Jesus as their own.

Who needs your intentional attention in this season of life? A coworker? A relative? A neighbor? Relational involvement is messy, so ask the Lord for His grace, patience, and forgiveness to fill your soul. Go the extra third and fourth mile to serve, even if someone takes advantage of your goodwill. It's better to take the risk to love than to withhold your affections from a hurting heart. If you receive a cold shoulder for your care, keep a warm heart. Love is the best relational investment.

We love like Jesus when we share our lives with people. We can eat together, travel together, worship together, pray together, study the Bible together, work together, play together, laugh together, and cry together. Perhaps you need to invite someone to live in your home for a defined period of time. It can be set up so they agree to abide by the ground rules of mutual respect, church attendance, and doing chores, and then understand they need an exit strategy after six months.

A Point to Ponder: Our homes can be incubators for relational development. An open home opens hearts to Jesus.

A solid relational investment plan requires a focus on faith. Equip another teachable soul in the tenets of trusting God. Pray with them, discuss the Bible with them, share your struggles with them, and talk of the Lord's faithfulness in your life. Or you may facilitate a book club with a few friends, join a small group from your church, or invest in a mission trip. Have a mutual fund of diverse friendships and you will never go broke relationally. Be grateful and give more than you receive in all relationships. Your relational investments will grow into true riches!

"We cared for you. Because we loved you so much, we were delighted to share with you not only the gospel of God but our lives as well" (1 Thessalonians 2:8).

Heavenly Father, show me whom I need to invest my life in,
with love and service, for Your sake.

TAKEAWAY: *Relational leaders invest their lives in others'*
lives.

Relational Adult Children Invest Time, Money, and Emotional Energy in Their Parents

For many years my father and I did not exactly see eye to eye, yet we valued our relationship over our differences. As adults we spent intentional time together and focused on getting to know one another better: What motivated us? What was our purpose? What did we fear, enjoy, and anticipate? Dad and I learned how to honor one another and in the process really understand each other.

George Bailey is the name of the Jimmy Stewart character in the beloved Christmas movie *It's a Wonderful Life*. It's a story of dreams, shattered hope, despair, revived hope, the significance of a life, and of a loving community. The movie provides a reminder of the more important things in life. Such is the story of my dad, another George Bailey, who went to be with the Lord in 2000.

As with most men, it was hard for Dad to share his inner feelings. But he desired for my brother Mitch and me to learn from his mistakes and successes. I appreciate much more now his sermon about eating healthy, getting exercise, and avoiding cigarettes. When I turned five, knowing I was a curious and bold child, he lit one up and had me smoke tobacco. Of course I turned first green, then pale, and proceeded to throw up. Emotionally and physically I was converted. By God's grace, to this day, I have not smoked another cigarette.

> **A Point to Ponder:** Difficult days are designed to draw us closer to Christ and to each other.

When I became a Christian in college, I wanted to express my newfound faith to those I loved and respected. Some were elated, others unsure, and a few thought I was off my rocker. Dad was in the third group. His response was, "Son, those church people have brainwashed you." He said, "I have my own way of thinking. Preachers used to come over to our house and preach to me—so don't preach to me." I learned quickly, the best thing I could do was live my Christianity before Dad by being a good son.

Two years after becoming a Christian, I excitedly told Dad I had been called to a vocation of Christian ministry. He deflated my bubble, saying, "Son, there is no money in that career choice, and whatever you do, don't go to Africa as a missionary!" However, I could tell Dad respected and loved me. He believed I would do what I thought was right, and that I would pursue my career calling with a 110-percent effort and abandonment.

Proximity can lead to closer relationships. In God's timing, I attended Southwestern Seminary in Fort Worth from 1982 to 1985. At that same time, Dad worked in our new city in the aerospace industry. Rita and I and Rebekah (then eight months old and the only grandchild) would go by for regular visits to see Dad and Pat, his wife. Our church was a mile from their apartment. I felt Dad and I grew much closer during that time. It was eerie how much I saw myself in him, and how much he saw himself in me. Though we didn't always agree, we respected and loved each other.

> **A Point to Ponder:** Bold leaders intentionally invest in others, especially in awkward situations.

Family, friends, and acquaintances prayed for Dad's spiritual and physical health over the years. One of those prayer requests was for Dad to know God in a personal way through Jesus Christ. It came after one of his near-death experiences. From his hospital bed, on the phone, he expressed to me how God had a purpose for him. Wisely, Dad recognized the Lord had allowed him to live for a reason. He believed in Christ and wanted to do His will.

Soon after coming into his newfound faith, Dad and Pat came to our home during Thanksgiving. The girls, Rita, and I gave him a Bible, which he gratefully cherished. He started attending a Bible study led by the pastor at a local church close to his home in Garland, Texas.

Pursuing a relationship with my dad was not always easy, but ultimately very fulfilling!

> **TAKEAWAY:** *Relational leaders honor their parents even when they are hard to honor.*

Relational Parents Teach Their Children the Way of Wisdom

"Pains as of a woman in childbirth come to him, but he is a child without wisdom; when the time arrives, he doesn't have the sense to come out of the womb" (Hosea 13:13).

As our four girls grew up, Rita and I tried to teach them ways to make wise decisions. At dinnertime we read the Proverbs together and discussed how to apply truth to our lives. Wise parents know the value of investing wisdom into their children. Here are some proven, fun, and creative ideas you can use with your child or grandchild.

Play and Eat Together

Finding time to corral the children for family devotions was an ongoing challenge. For a season, the four young girls, aged three to eleven, would act out Bible stories. Rebekah, the oldest, who loved to be in charge, was the director/actress and her three sisters the supporting cast. The ancient events came alive, and we all howled at the would-be Hollywood stars. As they grew older, we shifted to reading the Proverbs around the dinner table. Based on the day of the month, we would divide each chapter into verses. Each would read out loud and comment on how the Scripture applied to their life. It seemed the Lord would fit the individualized reading nicely to the life of the person quoting God's Word.

Tell Stories

Tell stories of individuals who made wise decisions and the positive effects that followed. Then contrast these uplifting illustrations with stories of those who chose an unwise path and suffered harm as a result. Stories stir the heart and illuminate the mind. We owe it to our offspring to engage them in conversations about real people. Otherwise they remain oblivious, in a bubble of unrealistic living. Wisdom comes by allowing young ones to spread their wings and begin decision-making while they still live under our roof.

> **A Point to Ponder:** A systematic approach to educating children in Scripture works the best.

Make Managing Money Interesting

Start out while they're young by helping them make money decisions. Show them the pattern of "share, save, and spend" from your own financial management. Then lead them to do the same. Watch them smile as they experience the joy of generosity. They will be able to save for something they want, purchasing their prize with cash. Let your own smart spending show a good example. You may become a recipient of its fruit as your child learns how to be a savvy shopper. Financial wisdom is a practical gift you can give to your children, thus training them (Ephesians 6:4).

Talk About How to Choose Friends

Good judgment in choosing friends is another facet of teaching your child the ways of wisdom. Make sure children understand the propensity to become like the people they "hang out" with. It's wise to choose friends whose faith is growing and robust. Be with friends who lift up, instead of those who pull down. It is unwise to flirt with friendships that dilute growth with God. Discuss why they need to avoid friendships that become a wedge between child and parent. Wisdom does not settle for the shallow acceptance of just any friend; it has a high standard for friendship. Challenge your children to pray for friends who complement their faith, who move them closer to their heavenly Father. Wise friends rub off on your children in wise ways.

Deposit God's Word into Their Hearts

Lastly, discuss with your child regularly the wisdom of God. He gives wisdom (Proverbs 2:6). Read with them from the Bible, and discuss the meaning of particular verses. Make Scripture conversation a natural part of your everyday spiritual diet. Take your Bible to church. Underline the phrases that leap from the page into your heart and mind, and over Sunday lunch talk about how they apply to your life. Ask your child to hold you accountable to the truth God is teaching you.

You cannot improve on the wisdom of the Lord. God's wisdom will follow your children the rest of their lives. It will be with them when you are absent. You can be at peace when you have a child who is wise in the ways of God. You are wise when your goal is to grow a wise child. Wise children have a much higher probability to grow into wise adults. Most of all teach them how to trust Jesus as their Lord and Savior. Toward the back of this book is a helpful resource, "How to Become a Disciple of Jesus Christ." Review these Scriptures with your child and trust the Holy Spirit will draw your son or daughter to Himself.

Children need to be taught wisdom. Yes, sometimes it's hard for them to grasp its meaning because of their age and stage in life. Wisdom comes through understanding and applying God's Word to life's experiences. Many individuals are limited in their perspective of both, so wisdom guides them away from unwise decision-making. Wisdom is one of the most wonderful gifts you can give your child. Be creative with your family to make education attractive, fun, and practical.

TAKEAWAY: *Relational leaders engage their children and grandchildren in the ways of wisdom.*

Healthy Marriage Partners Are Intentional in Their Relationship with Each Other and with God

"The Spirit makes it possible to submit humbly to one another out of respect for the Anointed [Christ]" (Ephesians 5:21 THE VOICE).

We told our children that next to them receiving the gift of salvation by faith in Jesus Christ, the second most important gift we could guide them toward was healthy marriages.

Our youngest daughter, Anna Grace, was married May 16, 2015. With very mixed emotions I gave her away. Along with my son-in-law Tripp, I officiated the ceremony. Rita and I wept tears of gratitude to God for giving us the opportunity to witness His work in Tyler and Anna's surrender to Christ and to one another. One hundred and seventy-five friends and family joined us at the Engine Room (a renovated cotton warehouse) to celebrate the Lord's faithfulness. While fresh on my mind, here are my reflections on how a wedding is preparation for marriage. It's a celebration and a consecration!

Submit to Christ

Jesus is the mediator between God and man, and He is the mediator in marriage. What does God's love require of us? This is the default question for a marriage that honors Jesus. Couples who worship Jesus together are drawn closer together. A husband and wife who love Christ have a deeper love for one another. Men and women who pray together tend to stay together. Their affections grow deeper because they focus their hearts on things above.

"Set your hearts on things above, where Christ is, seated at the right hand of God" (Colossians 3:1).

Read the Bible as God's Love Story

The Bible contains dos and don'ts we are wise to follow. It is a marriage manual that instructs us in how to have healthy emotional and relational interactions. But mostly, Holy Scripture is the simple story of our heavenly Father's love for us, and how we fit into that love story. The love story of our marriage is part of the Lord's larger story of unconditional love. God's Son died and rose again so we might die to ourselves and rise with Him. We are loved extravagantly so we might love extravagantly. Love in marriage covers sin and builds an enduring relationship.

"This is my prayer: that your love may abound more and more in knowledge and depth of insight, so that you may be able to discern what is best and may be pure and blameless for the day of Christ" (Philippians 1:9-10).

The Wedding Is an Event but Marriage Is a Lifelong Process

We spend time and money to plan an incredible wedding celebration, but it's just the launching pad for a lifelong marriage learning process. Premarital counseling from marriage mentors begins the process of how to communicate well, forgive fast, out-serve one another, and celebrate and embrace each other's differences. Each season of marriage requires new skills, so seek community with family and fellow Christ followers to create a healthy culture for nurturing your marriage. Be a student of your spouse. Learn how they like to be loved, as you both patiently stay in a prayerful process.

"Be devoted to one another in love. Honor one another above yourselves" (Romans 12:10).

Set a High Standard

As the world degrades marriage, Jesus followers are called to elevate marriage. Marriage is sacred. The lofty word picture of Jesus as our bridegroom and the church as His bride, is heaven's high standard for marriage. A husband gives himself up for his wife and loves her, as Christ gave Himself up for the church. A wife respects and follows her husband as she submits to and follows Christ. Even in our imperfection, we still aspire to God's perfect expectations for marriage. Humble hearts receive God's grace to do God's will. We receive the Lord's love, so we can love well.

"Husbands, love your wives, just as Christ loved the church and gave himself up for her" (Ephesians 5:25). "The wife must respect her husband" (Ephesians 5:33).

> **TAKEAWAY:** *Relational leaders view marriage as a laboratory for living out their faith.*

Relational Leaders Prayerfully and Wisely Approach Friendship at Work

"Faithful are the wounds of a friend, but the kisses of an enemy are deceitful" (Proverbs 27:6 NKJV).

As leaders, many of us want to be respected and liked by our fellow team members at work. But there is such a thing as becoming too familiar with our colleagues on the job. Relational leaders especially need to be cautious of not playing favorites and causing jealousy among the ranks.

When I became the new leader of our national sales team, my friend drew close to me. At first I was relieved he would offer his experience and expertise to assist me, but I soon learned there was more going on than just a desire to help. Because he had been first runner-up to my position, he was jealous and now jockeyed for control. If he couldn't have my job, he might convince me into following his wishes, thus leading without having responsibility. I soon discovered my friend had hijacked our relationship for his ambitious goals. I was stunned and angry. Soon we had a man-to-man discussion over his unhealthy influence. He backed off and I found new friends!

Lead first and be a friend second. An effective and efficient enterprise understands that leadership trumps friendship. As the old saying goes, "Lead, follow, or get out of the way." Wise and intentional leadership is necessary for the health of an organization, but leadership is watered down when friendships dictate strategic direction. Friendships should strengthen the team but not unduly dilute courageous leadership decisions.

If leaders are preoccupied with what their friends may think or do, then they risk diminishing a decision for the sake of sparing someone's feelings. Politics are not the plumb line. The values and principles of an organization are the standards by which leadership decisions should be made. Friendship can be a fruit of wise leadership, but it is not meant to drive it.

A Point to Ponder: Too-familiar friendships can lead to unhealthy influence.

Loyalty to friends is an important and valued attribute of an effective leader, but do not allow loyalty to cloud your understanding of what's best for the team. Sometimes the best thing you can do for the team and your friend is to either fire or reassign them. Be sure your leadership is grounded in principle so your friendships will not get in the way of doing what's right. Let a friend know up front how much you value them, but not to the detriment of what's best for the business or ministry.

"My son, do not make light of the Lord's discipline, and do not lose heart when he rebukes you, because the Lord disciplines the one he loves, and he chastens everyone he accepts as his son" (Hebrews 12:5-6).

A friend can be either the hardest or the easiest to lead. It all depends on expectations—yours and theirs. Does your friend perceive you as a partner or a boss? Lead first in humility, courage, and clarity. Let your friends know up front what you value as a leader and how they fit into the big picture of organizational success. Constantly ask, "What's best for the team?" instead of "What does my friend want?" Lead first by defining the role of friendship on the team, and keep leadership a priority by not playing favorites. This promotes teamwork and defuses jealousy.

Lastly, wise leaders make hard decisions, even when it adversely affects a friend. This protects the integrity of the organization. Paul felt this tension when he decided that his friend John Mark was not mature enough for the responsibility of a mission trip: "Barnabas wanted to take John, also called Mark, with them, but Paul did not think it wise to take him, because he had deserted them in Pamphylia and had not continued with them in the work" (Acts 15:37-38). Balancing leadership and friendship isn't always easy.

> **TAKEAWAY:** *Relational leaders do what's best for everyone instead of showing favoritism.*

Leading relationally is one of the most fulfilling aspects of serving as a wise leader. Whether at home or work, we have the opportunity to treat others like human beings with very real needs and wants, without compromising the vision and mission of the organization. There will always be a tension between valuing a relationship over results, but this is how we grow as wise leaders. Are you growing in your relational skills? Are you living in community and being challenged relationally? Wherever you are on the relational continuum of engaged or unengaged, stay in the relational game. By God's grace, grow a healthy marriage as a gift to your children's emotional well-being.

Summary of Chapter Four Takeaways

1. Relational leaders value relationships—sometimes more than measured results.

2. Relational leaders understand how relationships affect their quality of life.

3. Relational leaders value the eternal significance of relationships.

4. Relational leaders invest their lives in others' lives.

5. Relational leaders honor their parents even when they are hard to honor.

6. Relational leaders engage their children and grandchildren in the ways of wisdom.

7. Relational leaders view marriage as a laboratory for living out their faith.

8. Relational leaders do what's best for everyone instead of showing favoritism.

Chapter Five

Learning to Lead Like Jesus with Teachability

Show me your ways, LORD,
teach me your paths.
Guide me in your truth and teach me,
for you are God my Savior,
and my hope is in you all day long

Psalm 25:4-5

Being ignorant is not so much a shame,
as being unwilling to learn.

Benjamin Franklin

Jesus Was Teachable

J esus gave them this answer: 'Very truly I tell you, the Son can do nothing by himself; he can do only what he sees his Father doing, because whatever the Father does the Son also does'" (John 5:19).

Jesus was dependent on, and learned from, His heavenly Father. The Son never stopped learning from His Father. Christ confessed He could do nothing by Himself, but only what He saw His Father doing. So, tethered by trust in His Father, Jesus made sure to seek guidance from above before He made major moves below. Even in the middle of pressing needs, Jesus would disengage, depart to the mountains, and prayerfully seek His Father's heart. How much more should we also be desperately dependent on our heavenly Father?

What Does It Mean to Have a Teachable Heart?

"'Well said, teacher,' the man replied. 'You are right in saying God is one and there is no other but him.'…When Jesus saw that he had answered wisely, he said to him, 'You are not far from the kingdom of God'" (Mark 12:32,34).

Teachability is a primary fruit of humility. When we have an open heart to learn, we are in a position to receive wisdom from God and others. Jesus affirms a teachable heart, for He knows it has potential to learn and understand the things of God. A teachable heart is positioned to receive truth, and possesses an attitude consisting of more questions than answers.

A teachable heart recognizes truth when it comes knocking. It invites truth in to be examined, understood, and applied. Truth invigorates the teachable heart. There is a rush of spiritual adrenaline when truth intersects with an open mind and heart. Pride plateaus in its learning, but a teachable heart continues to scale the mountain of truth, understanding, and wisdom.

When the Lord discovers someone who is teachable, He calls him wise. Wisdom comes from God; therefore, a teachable heart learns the ways of God. The Holy Spirit facilitates teachability, as truth applied transforms behaviors and attitudes. Change that comes from the inside out makes us like Christ: humble, bold, wise, holy, gracious, encouraging, and faithful.

Change doesn't come easily, even if you understand God has your best interests in mind. But the transformation shows. Your character and behavior fall more in line with the life of Christ. Your spouse and children notice something different. You lead patiently and prayerfully instead of with fearful and intimidating tactics. Gain a teachable heart by first elevating your honor and worship of Almighty God.

A Point to Ponder: Pride plateaus in learning, but a teachable heart continues to scale the mountain of truth.

God is one. He is not one of many gods, but one God. He is not a mini-god, but the great and glorious God of the galaxies. God the Father, God the Son, and God the Holy Spirit are all one God. His oneness is to be worshipped and celebrated. Your love relationship with the one, true God is not to be rivaled by any other gods. Any acceptance of other gods is unacceptable to God. He is jealous for you. Your love for anyone or anything else will pale in relation to your love for Christ.

To love God is to make room for Him in all aspects of your life. You love Him when you love others, when you give sacrificially, when you strive for excellence in your work, and when you pray for and forgive others. Love is reciprocal—therefore, love Him and allow Him to love you.

Let Christ's expectations mold yours, because what He thinks trumps any other thinking. The Holy Spirit within you has the answers to the questions that consume your conscience. Listen to His internal promptings, not the external clamor. What you learned yesterday will be dwarfed by what you experience tomorrow. Know God, love God, and learn of Him. He affirms a teachable heart as one that fears the Lord. Wisdom in leadership fears God and follows His ways.

The Bible teaches, "Assemble the people—men, women, and children, and the foreigners living in your towns—so they can listen and learn to fear the Lord your God and follow carefully all the words of this law" (Deuteronomy 31:12).

TAKEAWAY: *Teachable leaders are ever learning the ways of the Lord.*

Teachable Leaders Become Eager Students in Stressful Situations

Without honest, open people in my life to teach me by their wise life choices, I would be a much lesser man today. I can hear good ideas and be moderately moved, but when I see an idea lived out it engages my heart, mind, and will in a way that moves me to be better. This is especially true when the fruit of wise decisions is attractive, as with my friend Greg and his compelling life for Christ.

I met Greg a few years back when he spoke at a businessmen's roundtable, where I was a member with 11 other men. We met for half a day each month, and our facilitator, Gayle, was Greg's mentor. Our speakers were always good, but Greg's story caused me to lean in and not be distracted by other things on my mind. In humility he told of his bold adventure of choosing family over career and character over compromise.

God often opens relational doors when we need to be blessed, so we can bless others. Early in our interactions Greg mentioned his desire, and the expectation of his company, for him to serve on a nonprofit board. Our organization, Ministry Ventures, was a perfect fit, with our blend of business and ministry culture. During the first three years Greg served as our financial/fund-raising committee chair, and the last three years he was our board chair. Like Jonathan and David we loved and respected each other. Our conversations were effortless; our values aligned; we were called by Christ and committed to His mission and vision for the ministry.

I was soon to become a student of Greg's ability to manage significant change. In my leadership experience I had never faced an economic recession like the one that rocked the world of for-profits and nonprofits in 2008. Our faith-based nonprofit had been thriving for nine years with a million-dollar budget, 80 percent dependent on donations. But with the sudden shift in our givers' net worth, income reduction, and in some cases loss of employment, we found ourselves needing to slash our operating expenses by 40 percent. Fortunately, we had no debt service to chew away our cash. Unfortunately, there was the agonizing experience of letting four team members go.

Greg was an uber-gifted administrator and equally skilled in relational dynamics. I never felt spoken down to, only lifted up by his language—expressed by his kind face and wise words. Each week we calendared a 30-minute call to review our cash position and to lovingly hold me accountable to my fund-raising calls, emails, and meetings. For two years we faithfully communicated with our weekly rhythm and boy, did the Lord honor our simple solution to a very overwhelming problem. Greg was my teacher during a difficult but teachable time for me.

Greg—like Aaron and Hur with Moses—placed the rock of his administrative gift underneath me so I could rest secure, then he lovingly held up my fatigued arms of fund-raising on those days when I didn't feel like going forward. Our gifts were different, but our Savior, our values, our community, and our common cause were the same. A wise leader depends on other wise leaders to coach them, especially during trials and tribulations.

> **TAKEAWAY:** *Teachable leaders learn from other leaders who complement their gifts and skills.*

Not So Fast!

Being an entrepreneur at heart, I've never met a new idea I didn't like. Our board of directors knows me well, and they have a favorite response to any of my new ideas: "Boyd, that sounds really cool and it's probably something we can consider next year, but in the meantime how are you doing on what we agreed on at our last meeting?" Ouch, and yes, they are right. Exactly what I *needed* to hear, but not what I *wanted* to hear. And friend, please don't play the "God card" with those who want the Lord's best for you. Don't say, "God wants me to do this; what do you think?" Why would anyone want to go against God? Better to say, "I'm praying about this idea; what do you think? I believe the Lord will validate His will through your counsel." Much better.

I get into trouble when I get ahead of the Lord. With my well-meaning excitement and energy I can forget to keep a long-term view on the wisdom of developing quality relationships, processes, and products. I was reminded of this recently in the vision for launching a Wisdom Hunters podcast. Naively, I thought all it would take was a few phone calls, one meeting to learn how to record, finding someone to upload the recording to iTunes, and we would be good to go. Not so fast, Boyd!

What I quickly discovered was I needed a gifted producer, a co-host, a compelling script, a content timeline, quality recording equipment, a budget, background music, a soothing voice for an introduction and a conclusion, an experienced editor, and a robust digital marketing plan. Wow. Was I ever ill-prepared to enjoy a quality outcome. But fortunately the Lord eventually sent us all the valuable ingredients for a compelling podcast program. It took four times as long as I anticipated to create, and the cost was three times what I estimated. But boy, was it worth the wait to take the time to focus on quality, instead of releasing an inferior listener experience. A focus on quality leads to quantity results. A wise leader waits for the best time for a new idea.

TAKEAWAY: *Teachable leaders are careful not to get ahead of themselves or those they lead.*

A Teachable Leader Is Ready to Receive the Truth

"I have much more to say to you, more than you can now bear. But when he, the Spirit of truth, comes, he will guide you into all the truth" (John 16:12-13).

A heart prepared to receive truth is rare and valuable to the recipient. Jesus knew the limitations of the disciples' ability to understand and apply truth, since the Holy Spirit had not yet come, as He would at Pentecost. In the same way, the Spirit prepares our hearts to receive all types of truth: Encouragement, comfort, and corrective words are all necessary. Notice how Jesus stated the role of the Spirit in guiding the disciples into all truth.

I am not always ready to receive what the Lord wants to show me or teach me. It may mean my heart needs to be humbled, my mind needs understanding, or my experience needs to catch up with my knowledge. My loving heavenly Father knows the best timing, so I don't become proud over success or humiliated over failure. I am learning to trust Him and stay ready for the next step. In the meantime, I will remain faithful where I am.

Jesus knew the disciples were at a disadvantage—they had not yet received the Holy Spirit. When pilots become instrument rated, they are certified to fly a plane by instruments alone when maneuvering through clouds. Similarly, the disciples would soon have the Spirit of God to guide them through the clear or cloudy days to come. Out of compassion, the Lord did not place more on His followers than they could handle. Information only frustrates if there is no clarity about what to do next. The Spirit guides us.

"I gave you milk, not solid food, for you were not yet ready for it" (1 Corinthians 3:2).

How is the Lord stretching and growing your faith? Perhaps His Spirit is telling you to remain faithful with the little things, so you can be trusted with larger opportunities. A small job done well is the bridge to a bigger job. God gives you just what you need when you need it, and not before. If you prematurely take matters into your own hands, you may get what you want, but forfeit your heavenly Father's reward.

By God's grace, grow in patience and perseverance. Take time to learn the ways of Jesus by following the Spirit of Truth with a humble heart. What is unclear becomes lucid as you wait on the Lord. Submit to the Lord and become a lifelong learner. Aspire to learn from the Spirit so you can be led by the Spirit. The Holy Spirit directs a life in motion, so stay in the process of proceeding through the unknown. The promised land is acquired by those who learn and apply their heavenly Father's promises. Wisdom in leadership allows the Lord to prepare them to receive truth.

"Whoever can be trusted with very little can also be trusted with much" (Luke 16:10).

Heavenly Father, I trust You to get me ready for what You will have me be and do.

TAKEAWAY: *Teachable leaders prepare heart and mind to receive the truth.*

A Teachable Leader Waits on God's Timing

Andy Stanley tells the following story about Truett Cathy, the founder of Chick-fil-A. Back in the 1990s there was a company called Boston Chicken that eventually became Boston Market. This was Chick-fil-A's first serious competition because they were also in the fast-food chicken business. They were similar in what they offered and how they presented themselves, unlike the other fast-food chains. And Boston Market had huge expansion plans. In fact, they wanted to have sales of $1 billion by the year 2000. So the Chick-fil-A insiders were a little nervous about this. This was their first real competition for the same customers. They began to feel pressure. Chick-fil-A began conversations about how to grow bigger and faster.

So, as the story goes from a Chick-fil-A vice president, the whole situation culminated in a boardroom with all the VPs and marketing people going back and forth around the table. How do we get bigger faster? How do we compete with Boston Market? Truett was down at the end of the table, and he was very, very quiet. In fact, it didn't even look like he was engaged in the meeting at all. And then suddenly, uncharacteristically, Truett started banging his fist on the table until he had everybody's attention. I guess he didn't have a bell he could ring.

He said, "Gentlemen, I am sick and tired of hearing you talk about us getting bigger." And then he paused. He went on, "What we need to be talking about is getting better." And then he gave us the quote that I wrote down and hung in my office. He said, "If we get better, our customers will demand that we get bigger."

That shifted the whole conversation. It was a defining moment in their strategy. And just anecdotally, in 2000, Boston Market filed for bankruptcy. It was that same year that Chick-fil-A hit $1 billion in sales for the first time. That's how great leaders think. They just shift the paradigm. They see through a different filter. How do we make it better? If we make it better, we believe our customers will force us to get bigger.

TAKEAWAY: *Teachable leaders are patient to make things better, before becoming bigger.*

A Teachable Leader Is an Authentic Follower of Christ

"His disciples asked him what this parable [the Sower] meant… 'This is the meaning of the parable: The seed is the word of God'" (Luke 8:9,11).

Most importantly, a teachable leader needs to be a true follower of Jesus. Where are you in your faith? The following is not meant to be a short list of neat categories for us to judge ourselves and each other, but a way to better understand Jesus's parable. Ponder and pray over the four spiritual heart conditions Christ described:

1. The Almost Christian

"Those along the path are the ones who hear, and then the devil comes and takes away the word from their hearts, so that they may not believe and be saved" (Luke 8:12).

An almost Christian hears the truth, but the enemy—the devil—quickly snatches the Word of God from their heart and replaces it with lies. A hard heart is unable to receive Scripture into its proud, barren soil. Only by humility and faith is it softened. A teachable heart treasures the truth and protects it from Satan's deceptive tactics of doubt. The only hope for this unsaved soul is to surrender to Jesus in contrition.

2. The Convenient Christian

"Those on the rocky ground are the ones who receive the word with joy when they hear it, but they have no root. They believe for a while, but in the time of testing they fall away" (Luke 8:13).

"If it's convenient, I'll say I am a Christian; if it's not convenient, I'll act like I'm not a Christian." This is the motto of men and women who only use Christianity to further their self-interest. When they first hear about Jesus, joy is the reaction, but when their emotional foundation is tested, they fall away—faithless. They may say the right words or even attend church, but their hearts are far from God. A convenient Christian is a counterfeit. They have no true belief rooted in conviction.

3. The Immature Christian

"The seed that fell among thorns stands for those who hear, but as they go on their way they are choked by life's worries, riches, and pleasures, and they do not mature" (Luke 8:14).

Immature Christians are still infants in their comprehension of righteousness. Worry, money, and pleasures have all stunted their growth in God's grace. They know the Lord—they have been saved—but they only snorkel at the surface of their salvation. These babes have yet to scuba dive, plunging into the depths of God's love, comfort, and fellowship of suffering. Mature faith perseveres through pain and has the discipline to enjoy pleasures without worshipping them.

4. The Growing Christian

"The seed on good soil stands for those with a noble and good heart, who hear the word, retain it, and by persevering produce a crop" (Luke 8:15).

Growing Christians guard their hearts with the peace of God. Suffering softens their hearts and success humbles their hearts. Seeds of truth establish deep roots. The Word of God rarely grows old, only richer. Wisely, they discover new ways to be more like Jesus, growing a crop of character, with a hearty harvest of souls. Growing Christians retain truth by meditating on, memorizing, and applying the Bible. They stop growing when they stop breathing. Growth means change, change takes grace, grace comes from God, and God gives grace to the humble!

"He [God] gives grace generously. As the Scriptures say, 'God opposes the proud but gives grace to the humble'" (James 4:6 NLT).

Honestly ask yourself if you are a genuine follower of Christ. If not, you can kneel down right now, repent of your sins, and confess faith in Jesus Christ as your Savior and Lord.

> *Heavenly Father, by Your grace, make me into a growing Christian. In Jesus's name, Amen.*

TAKEAWAY: *Teachable leaders have authentic faith that challenges others to have the same.*

A Teachable Leader Learns to Anticipate and Overcommunicate

Let's look at a home life example of how we can better plan, manage the calendar, and be hospitable without stressing out anyone.

For me marriage is a daily exercise in seeking to make sure what I've said makes sense. Just because it's clear in my head does not mean my words make it just as clear in Rita's mind. One day I energetically mentioned the idea of inviting a couple to dinner. We could all get to know each other better and have a fun time. She liked the idea and wanted to think about it, as we were cautious not to overcommit our calendar. After a few days we both determined two weeks out would be the best time to be with our new friends. In my naturally aggressive approach, I invited the nice couple to our home to grill out and have some meaningful conversation.

Rita looked stunned and surprised when I told her about extending the invitation, "Why didn't you talk to me first?" she said, feeling disrespected. I stammered out, "I did—remember, we waited a few days to confirm the calendar and then we both agreed it was a good time to hang out together." "Yes, but we didn't decide on having dinner at our home. The house is a mess and it's so stressful to prepare, cook, and clean up. Let's just meet them for dinner at a quiet restaurant and we can enjoy each other's company without the hassle of anyone having to host."

I had assumed having our new friends in our home was the best and most convenient way to enjoy a nice meal together. I forgot to ask Rita her preference and opinion. I am learning to review the details of a generally agreed-upon idea to assure all parties are on the same page. It's better when I take the time to talk through with Rita the reasons why I would like to entertain at home (warmth, relaxation, and allowing the couple to better know us), but also respect her reasons for wanting to eat out (convenience, less hassle, and the ability to be present in the conversation, not distracted by serving others). Wisdom in leadership thoroughly confirms the details before implementing the plan.

TAKEAWAY: *Teachable leaders grow in their skill to communicate clearly, creatively, and often.*

A Teachable Leader Is Willing to Leave the Comfortable for the Uncomfortable

"By faith Abraham, when called to go to a place he would later receive as his inheritance, obeyed and went, even though he did not know where he was going" (Hebrews 11:8).

Very early in my walk with Christ I was faced with a big decision to move or to stay put. The Lord stretched our faith during that season of transition. I had only been a Christian two years. A friend taught on the above verse from Hebrews, and my heart was strangely moved by the Holy Spirit to go into full-time ministry. That meant attending seminary (graduate theological school) so I would have the knowledge and skills to speak, lead, and write well. Rita had never lived out of Marshall County, Alabama. We went to Texas not really knowing where we were going or what we would do, but the Lord clarified each step along the way. We learned to obey God and trust He would give us the wisdom and relationships to do His will.

It is time to go when God says so, even though you are not sure where you are going. Abraham was a "friend of God" (James 2:23 NASB) who trusted the heart of God. He was secure in his faith, knowing his heavenly Father would not lead him astray. Are you okay with nothing but the call of Christ as your next step? Is He calling you out of your comfort zone to a new level of faith and obedience? Wisdom in leadership listens for a clear and compelling call from the Lord.

A Point to Ponder: Teachable leaders are willing to step out in faith even when they are unsure of where they are going.

Maybe God wants you to move with your company so your career can become the means of funding your passion for missions. Locals in foreign countries are keenly interested in teachers, housewives, doctors, bankers, and business persons who visit their worlds. The marketplace is your ministry. It validates your value and confirms your character. The Lord will use your obedience to encourage the faith of others and especially the faith of your family.

The faith of parents often instills the blessing of obedience on their posterity. When your teenage son sees you say "yes" to Christ's challenge, he will be more likely to say "yes" to wisdom when faced with issues of trust. Your daughter will not soon forget your family's earnest prayers as you sought God's best and obeyed. Parents who obey God's call create the same expectation for their children, so follow the Lord for them.

The call of Christ leads to His blessing on earth and in heaven. It may mean prosperity; it may mean poverty; or it may mean something between. The most important reward is that of your eternal inheritance. Leave a legacy of loving the Lord, and you will have loved your children. Follow Him faithfully and there is a much higher probability they will as well. Is it time to go? Then go with your best friend, Jesus. Wisdom in leadership is willing to take Spirit-led risks.

"God's intimate friendship blessed my house" (Job 29:4).

Where is Christ calling me to a higher level of faith and obedience?

TAKEAWAY: *Teachable leaders are willing to move out of their comfort zones and learn new things.*

A Teachable Leader Reads and Comprehends Meaningful Books

To have assigned readings in meaningful books is one way to build a routine of rich discussion on interesting topics. A book club is one way to accomplish this goal. Simply ask three other people who want to learn to join you once a month.

I am a member of three book clubs. One studies classics; we have met for three and a half years. The second is three years old; we read biographies, business books, and leadership books. This year I started a virtual book club (by video conference) that also studies the classics (selfishly, the books I've already read!).

Each of these has an organized format. For the first classic book study we take 90 minutes over lunch: 30 minutes to catch up on each other's lives, 60 minutes to discuss the book, and a few minutes at the end to rate the book on a scale from one to five, with five being the highest. The second group takes 60 minutes, from 7:45 to 8:45 am: 15 minutes to catch up and 45 minutes to discuss the book. We use the same 60-minute format for the virtual book club. I always gain much more from the group experience than I would from just reading on my own. Iron does sharpen iron (Proverbs 27:17) when others challenge our thinking. Check out the appendix for a suggested list from my friend Ken Boa.

TAKEAWAY: *Teachable leaders discuss timeless books and ideas with others.*

A Teachable Leader Never Stops Learning

"Say to wisdom, 'You are my sister,' and call understanding your nearest kin" (Proverbs 7:4 NKJV).

Leaders are learners. When they stop learning they cease to lead wisely. Continuing education is essential for leaders who want to think ahead and execute effectively. The leader who does not assess the facts of a situation and operate in reality is not in a good position. But the leader who is ever learning lives a circumspect and wise life.

A leader continually asks questions like, "How can we better understand what the customer wants and needs?" "How can I get out of the way as the leader, and support the team for it to be successful?" "How can our organization go from good to great by integrating and sustaining our industry's best practices?" Leaders who learn ask the right questions, get the most accurate answers, and are able to make the wisest decisions.

"Jehoshaphat also said to the king of Israel, 'First seek the counsel of the LORD'" (1 Kings 22:5).

Leaders learn by listening to the Lord and the wisdom found in His Word. Teachability is not a one-time educational event but requires the ongoing purging of pride, pretense, and prayerlessness. Wisdom becomes like a beloved sister to whom you go for counsel. The Holy Bible is your armor against the assault of unwise thinking.

A Point to Ponder: Teachable leaders listen to the Lord first when seeking the wise choice.

Read, study, and apply the Word of God regularly to your life. Read books that highlight bright examples of leaders worth emulating. Learn by listening to teachers who communicate truth with clarity and conviction. Learn from your mistakes, and do not repeat them. Our relationships are laboratories for learning. Learn how to forgive with your family; learn how to serve with your friends; and learn how to love with your enemies. A wise and teachable leader never stops learning.

"If you have any encouragement from being united with Christ, if any comfort from his love, if any common sharing in the Spirit, if any tenderness and compassion, then make my joy complete by being like-minded, having the same love, being one in spirit and of one mind" (Philippians 2:1-2).

What life lessons do I need to currently learn so the Lord can entrust me with further educational opportunities?

TAKEAWAY: *Teachable leaders love God with their minds by learning and applying His Word.*

On a scale of one to ten, with ten being "extremely teachable," where do you land? Where do you see an immediate need for growth? Keep trusting God and be open to learn and grow.

Summary of Chapter Five Takeaways

1. Teachable leaders are ever learning the ways of the Lord.

2. Teachable leaders learn from other leaders who complement their gifts and skills.

3. Teachable leaders are careful not to get ahead of themselves or those they lead.

4. Teachable leaders prepare heart and mind to receive the truth.

5. Teachable leaders are patient to make things better before becoming bigger.

6. Teachable leaders have authentic faith that challenges others to have the same.

7. Teachable leaders grow in their skill to communicate clearly, creatively, and often.

8. Teachable leaders are willing to move out of their comfort zones and learn new things.

9. Teachable leaders discuss timeless books and ideas with others.

10. Teachable leaders love God with their minds by learning and applying His Word.

Chapter Six

Learning to Lead Like Jesus with Discipline

*For the moment all discipline seems
painful rather than pleasant,
but later it yields the peaceful fruit of righteousness
to those who have been trained by it.*

Hebrews 12:11 ESV

*You must arrange your days so that you are
experiencing deep contentment,
joy, and confidence in your everyday life with God.*

John Ortberg

Jesus Was Disciplined

Then Jesus was led by the Spirit into the wilderness to be tempted by the devil. After fasting for forty days and forty nights, he was hungry. The tempter came to him and said, 'If you are the Son of God, tell these stones to become bread.' Jesus answered, 'It is written: "Man shall not live on bread alone, but on every word that comes from the mouth of God"'" (Matthew 4:1-4).

Jesus was able to leave His regular routine, get away, and get with God. He did not allow His service for the Father to substitute for His communion with the Father. As He disciplined His body, emotions, soul, and will for a 40-day fast, He was tempted by the devil. He had hid God's Word in His heart, so He was able to answer His adversary's accusations with truth. Jesus's prior discipline to memorize Scripture supported His present discipline of fasting and praying. The Spirit uses our discipline to defend us against our adversaries, and ultimately defeat the devil's temptations.

What Is Discipline?

What comes to mind when you think of the word *discipline*? Probably...sacrifice, hard work, no grace, no fun, and white-knuckled determination. The Merriam-Webster definition is "punishment; instruction; training that corrects, molds or perfects the mental facilities or moral character."[7]

These ideas and definitions do not necessarily inspire me to become disciplined as a devoted and loving disciple of Jesus. I need a different approach, a way to experience God that is as routine as bathing, or flossing and brushing my teeth.

Learning to Manage Routines Instead of Dreading Discipline

What if we think of discipline as managing our good routines?

Recently I changed my morning shaving routine. For 37 years I first shaved off my 24-hour stubble and then showered. My logic was to shave first, then shower so I could wash off the shaving cream. It makes sense, right? However, over the years I got a lot of nicks and cuts that I accepted as part of the shaving experience—an experience that included sticking moistened pieces of tissue on my red-splotched chin, and looking like I had been the loser in a 15-round boxing match! One day I was complaining about frequent violent encounters with my razor, when Rita recommended I shower first then shave. "This moistens your face and causes your stubble to stand more erect," she explained.

You may ask, how do you change a 37-year-old habit? One way is to anticipate lesser pain by making a small adjustment in your routine. And, would you believe it, the following 90 days there were no cuts, a closer, cleaner shave, and no needless facial embarrassment. So then I thought, *Boyd, what other routines need to be adjusted—even slightly tweaked—to experience a much better outcome, even lesser pain?*

Maybe we can manage our routines around the spiritual discipline of soul care. My thought is that the more we build our motivation around caring for our soul, the more we will have the understanding and focus to follow God and His will for our lives. If we invest first in a healthy soul, we will be able to support and care for a healthy body, emotions, and mind. Disciplined soul care begins with a desire for God's will, death to our own wills, and coming alive for Christ.

"I desire to do your will, my God; your law is within my heart" (Psalm 40:8). "Take delight in the LORD, and he will give you the desires of your heart" (Psalm 37:4).

> **TAKEAWAY:** *Disciplined leaders establish regular routines that grow their devotion to Jesus.*

Disciplined Leaders Surrender Their Kingdom to God's Kingdom

"Very truly I tell you, unless a kernel of wheat falls to the ground and dies, it remains only a single seed. But if it dies, it produces many seeds" (John 12:24).

I recently ran across this very clever, yet convicting parable about how we organize our lives in ways that may or may not reflect the Lord's priorities.

A Modern Parable: A Kingdom of Acorns

Once upon a time, in a not-so-faraway land, there was a kingdom of acorns—a myriad of acorns nestled at the foot of a grand, old oak tree.

Since the citizens of this kingdom were modern and fully Westernized acorns, they went about their business with purposeful energy. Since they were mid-life, baby-boomer acorns, they took a lot of self-help courses. There was a seminar called "Getting All You Can Out of Your Shell." There were woundedness and recovery groups for acorns who had been bruised in their original fall from the tree. There were retreats and spas for oiling and polishing those shells, and various acorn-opathic therapies to enhance longevity and well-being.

One day in the midst of this kingdom there suddenly appeared a knotty little stranger, apparently dropped out of the blue by a passing bird. He was odd: capless and dirty. He made an immediate negative impression on his fellow acorns. Crouched beneath the oak tree, he stammered out a strange and wild tale. Pointing upward at the tree, he spoke to all that would listen to him and said, "We...are...that!"

Delusional thinking, obviously, the other acorns concluded.

But one or two of them continued to engage him in conversation. "So tell us, how would we become that tree?" "Well," said he, pointing downward, "it has something to do with going into the ground, and cracking open the shell." "Insane!" they responded. "Totally morbid! Why, then we wouldn't be acorns anymore!"[8]

Clever and convicting. What is your application from the acorn story?

Which kingdom has your loyalty? Your tiny acorn kingdom or God's massive kingdom of trees?

The psalmist described how a tree rooted by life-giving water yields luscious fruit: "That person is like a tree planted by streams of water, which yields its fruit in season and whose leaf does not wither—whatever they do prospers" (Psalm 1:3).

> **TAKEAWAY:** *Disciplined leaders plant their lives by the water of God's Word and bear good fruit.*

Disciplined Leaders Are Inspired by Their Devotion to Christ

"His heart was devoted to the ways of the LORD" (2 Chronicles 17:6).

What is the difference between devotion and discipline? Is one more valuable than the other? Devotion is an overriding commitment to Christ and His way of doing things. It engages the heart and mind in learning the ways of the Lord and then applying them. Devotion must be the driving force behind a disciple's faith for them to persevere in Christ's call on their life. Your devotion to God dictates how you will live your life.

Discipline, on the other hand, is the ability to stay focused on the task at hand. It finishes the assignment or completes the course. A disciplined person trains to improve their strength and self-control. They are religious at carrying out routines, fulfilling checklists, and getting things done. Discipline is designed to grow your faith, with regular readings from God's Word, and engaging prayers of praise, thanksgiving, confession, and repentance.

However, make sure your discipline is driven by your devotion or you become judgmental and insensitive. Devotion to Christ first keeps your heart of faith full of grace and truth. Discipline without devotion is like a billowing cloud that gives no refreshing rain. It can become so rigid in its rules that it causes decent and devoted people to flee. So, apply devotion to both God and people. "Be devoted to one another in love. Honor one another above yourselves" (Romans 12:10).

Furthermore, direct your passionate devotion to focus on one thing. Like Paul, learn to channel all your energies into one endeavor, and see it through to the end. "Paul devoted himself exclusively to preaching, testifying to the Jews that Jesus was the Messiah" (Acts 18:5). It is better to complete one task than to start a dozen and leave them all undone. Indeed, your devotion to Christ determines your discipline over the long term. Keep this your motivation, and discipline will follow. A heart devoted to the Lord's ways does not stray.

Is my heart devoted to the ways of the Lord? Does my discipline flow from my devotion to Christ?

TAKEAWAY: *Disciplined leaders are wise to not substitute their warm devotion for cold discipline.*

A Disciplined Leader Has a Growing Desire for Disciplined Soul Care

So, what are some ways we can grow our desire for soul care around helpful routines? One way is to get away and get quiet before the Lord in His creation.

Several years ago I was recovering from early-stage prostate cancer. My mind, heart, and body needed an infusion from God. My soul needed to catch up with my frantic pace. I needed silence in order to manage my noisy life. My energy to lead was spent. Emotionally and physically exhausted, but spiritually expectant, I started my silent, listening prayer exercise at the Bethlehem Retreat House at The Abbey of the Genesee (near Rochester, New York).

Here is a journal excerpt from my precious time with a monk, as I experienced my heavenly Father's love:

> Just met with Brother Earl Marcellus. He was like Jesus, having served as a Cistercian monk since 1954 and at the Abbey of the Genesee since 1964. His spirit was humble, humorous, and disarming. He struggled with a scratchy throat and was somewhat hard of hearing, but we communicated just fine. I thanked Brother Marcellus for his time and asked him for his wisdom on a matter. He said he had no wisdom, but the Holy Spirit would guide our conversation.
>
> In a raised voice, I said, "Our heavenly Father is calling me into a deeper understanding and experience in grace and humility." I wondered from his years of walking with Christ what advice and counsel he would give me on how to grow in grace and humility with our Lord. The next words out of his mouth surprised me: "You need to be a saint!" Not just an ordinary saint, and certainly not a saint who barely gets into heaven, but a saint who seeks to be holy as God is holy. Yes, obey His commands, for Jesus said that if we loved Him we would obey Him. And that those who wish to be called His brothers or sisters hear His Word and do it.

TAKEAWAY: *Disciplined leaders are influenced by other disciplined leaders.*

Brother Marcellus stressed the critical discipline of thanking God, moment by moment, for what I encounter in everyday life. If a mosquito swirls around my head, thank Him; if my college football team loses, thank Him; if I contract cancer, thank Him. I told Brother Marcellus I had experienced early-stage prostate cancer and grown closer to Christ more than ever before. He continued by explaining that God wants 100 percent of our attachments to be from His will and not our will. We can become too attached to something that is not from God's will, and then become angry when it is disrupted or challenged. By thanking God in all things, we are released from anger or affection; we are released from that object of our attachment.

Brother Marcellus said, "Boyd, do you want to know what it means to walk in grace and humility with Jesus Christ?" "Yes," I said. He continued, "Any time you are hurt or offended, the time it takes for you to thank God and forgive is an indicator of how close your walk is with Christ."

He held up his two bony pointer fingers six inches apart, and slowly moved them together. "Some have a lifetime of unforgiveness, and they die in bitterness. For others, it takes years to forgive; for others, months; for others, weeks; for others, days; for others, hours; for others, minutes; for others, seconds; and for those whose walk is closest to Christ, their forgiveness and thanksgiving is simultaneous to the offense." I was breathless. My soul stimulated, my emotions elevated, I asked my heavenly Father to remove any unforgiveness or ingratitude lingering in my heart. I felt free indeed!

TAKEAWAY: *Disciplined leaders forgive quickly and remain grateful to God.*

I thanked Brother Marcellus for his time. He gave me an extra ten minutes, for a total of 40.

I asked if I could pray for him. "Of course," he said, and then he expounded beautifully for another five minutes on the art of continuous prayer. He said, "Boyd, instead of talking to ourselves during the day, we need to take those same conversations and have them with our heavenly Father. That is prayer! So, when we are unsure, we ask Him about it. When we are angry, we work it out with Him, by thanking

Him and processing with Him." So, I prayed a silent prayer for Brother Marcellus, thanking God for him and the wisdom our Lord spoke through him to me.

Humbled to be in the room with true greatness, I asked him to pray over me a blessing. "Of course, Boyd. I'm honored to pray for you," he replied. I knelt in front of him, by his chair next to the small couch where I was sitting. It was like I was in the presence of Jesus, and I was!

Brother Marcellus stood over me and prayed this blessing: "Blessed Father, bless your son Boyd with Your great love. Fill Him with Your Spirit to know and obey Your will. May his life bring glory to You. And yes, Father, may he bear abundant fruit for Your glory. Amen."

His somewhat trembling hands touched my head. Yes, I had been touched by God through His godly servant! I stood up and hugged his frail, faithful body. I felt my heavenly Father's hug.

I had asked Brother Marcellus and the Lord for a deeper understanding of wisdom and humility, and for 40 minutes this man of God, this great saint of Jesus, lived, breathed, talked, and prayed like one full of the Spirit, full of grace and wisdom. He modeled the way right in front of me. Thank You, Jesus!

Majestically, I felt my soul carried out as if on the wings of angels. In a surreal mood, I made my way to the men's room and wept. I prayed, "Dear Lord, I want to be a selfless, humble, grace-filled saint like Brother Marcellus. Thank You for allowing him to be Jesus, for me, today. Thank You, heavenly Father, for speaking Your Word through Your servant!"

TAKEAWAY: *Disciplined leaders walk with wise leaders, apply their words, and copy their actions.*

Disciplined Leaders Become Fluent in Silence, the Language of God

A five-day silent retreat is not required if you want to hear from God or grow a disciplined walk with Christ. But if you can afford this investment of time, you will not be disappointed. I talk more about this experience on video at www.wisdomhunters.com. Remember, prayer saves us time by aligning our agendas with God's agenda. Prayer fuels our faith and empowers our work. Creatively manage your routines around experiencing the Lord in prayer, Bible reflection, and worship. There is a universal language the Lord speaks, and it is silence. Quietly read these next few pages. Perhaps turn off your phone. Listen: The Lord is speaking.

"This is what the Sovereign LORD, the Holy One of Israel, says: 'In repentance and rest is your salvation, in quietness and trust is your strength, but you would have none of it'...Yet the LORD longs to be gracious to you; therefore he will rise up to show you compassion. For the LORD is a God of justice. Blessed are all who wait for him!" (Isaiah 30:15,18).

Isaiah described the Sovereign Lord's heart for His people to enjoy their salvation through repentance, rest, quietness, and trust. These attributes were the fuel for their strength. Though they initially resisted, the Lord remained compassionate to remind them of His justice. If they would wait for Him, He would fulfill His promises to His people. Blessings come when we wait for God's best. When burdens beset us, we don't panic and act like we are alone, but quietly trust.

Silence is the soul's remedy for spiritual fatigue. Be still.

Are you becoming fluent in God's language of silence? Are you able to comprehend what Christ says to your heart through Holy-Spirit-inspired Scripture, and through His creation? Be still and know He is God. Be still and know He is. Be still and know Him. Be still and know. Be still. Be. This is something to be learned, just like any new language. A linguist devotes their skill and energy to learn a new language, and in time is conversationally fluent. So, stay immersed in the process. Your heavenly Father is patient to work with you where you are. Also learn from sages who speak the language of silence fluently. God's language is not to be taken lightly. Silence your heart, and you will grow into a disciple who finishes well.

"Be still and know that I am God" (Psalm 46:10).

"He makes me lie down in green pastures, he leads me beside quiet waters, he refreshes my soul. He guides me along the right paths for his name's sake" (Psalm 23:2-3).

"In repentance and rest is your salvation, in quietness and trust is your strength" (Isaiah 30:15).

"Learn in quietness and full submission" (1 Timothy 2:11).

> **TAKEAWAY:** *Disciplined leaders learn to listen to the Lord and receive His sweet love.*

Hurry: The Enemy of Being Still and Listening

There seems to be an enemy to every good thing we experience, and hurry is certainly the enemy of being still and knowing God. So, what are some ways we can slow down our lives, especially with our families?

I love John Ortberg's book *Soul Keeping*, where he quotes his mentor Dallas Willard: "Hurry is the great enemy of spiritual life in our day. You must ruthlessly eliminate hurry from your life."

John goes on, "The space where we find rest and healing for our souls is solitude...My mind may be obsessed with idols; my will may be enslaved to habits; my body may be consumed with appetites. But my soul will never find rest until it rests in God."[9]

> **TAKEAWAY:** *Disciplined leaders are relentless in their pursuit of being still and knowing God.*

Disciplined Parents Practice Slow Parenting

"Fathers, do not provoke your children to anger [do not exasperate them to the point of resentment...], but bring them up [tenderly, with lovingkindness] in the discipline and instruction of the Lord" (Ephesians 6:4 AMP).

Recently, I enjoyed watching our four-year-old grandson at a swimming lesson. On our walk back through the parking lot to the car, we encountered a bright yellow speed bump—two feet wide, ten feet long, and one foot high. It was perfect for a pretend walk on an imagined circus high wire. Our daring four-year-old and his two-year-old brother drifted toward the speed bump with Mom and Dad close by. The parents patiently watched the boys walk briskly across the asphalt adventure. With only a five-minute delay, we all enjoyed a moment—a memory together. Mom and Dad allowed a speed bump to slow them down and joyfully experienced their children.

The apostle Paul had no children of his own that we know of, but he was a student of parenting. He knew from keen observation that a child needs spontaneous opportunities to express their childlike interests. A forceful and inflexible parent risks running their son or daughter through their childhood with only a blur of activities. A child who is unable to slow down and be a child can become irritated, exasperated, even resentful. Parents who allow for unhurried time with their children model God's patient love. The Lord's instruction is best received with slow parenting.

"It has given me great joy to find some of your children walking in the truth, just as the Father commanded us" (2 John 1:4).

A Point to Ponder: Parents who trust the Lord are able to slow down and allow joy to catch up.

Do you occasionally find yourself worshipping at the altar of hurry? You discover your hyperactive schedule competes with quality family time. Hurry is not a badge of good parenting, but a confession of an out-of-control calendar. An out-of-control calendar can lead to an out-of-control child. Perhaps you could declare one day a week to be technology free. Use that time to act out Bible stories and play board games. Take a walk after dinner and pray for a friend who needs Jesus. Enjoy at least one meal a day with everyone together. Slow parenting requires bold planning.

One sport or hobby a year per child can be plenty. When you slow down as a parent, you can get up to speed in really understanding each child's unique needs and wants. No one feels left out when you have quality time with each one. Quality interaction with your child flows from unhurried blocks of time. Most of all, slow down to be with your Savior. Christ grants clarity and confidence in an unhurried prayer time. Your soul reveals who you are; your heart receives strength for life's journey; your mind is renewed by truth; and your will aligns with God's will. Slow parenting is a picture of the Lord's loving patience. Slow down to invest in what's best!

"The LORD, the LORD, the compassionate and gracious God, slow to anger, abounding in love and faithfulness, maintaining love to thousands, and forgiving wickedness, rebellion and sin" (Exodus 34:6-7).

Heavenly Father, give me the patience to have unhurried time with You and with my child.

TAKEAWAY: *Disciplined leaders take the time to be present and to live in the present.*

Disciplined Leaders Practice Business Discipline in Their Work

"Prepare your work outside and get it ready for yourself in the field; afterward build your house and establish a home" (Proverbs 24:27 AMP).

The last area of discipline I would like to discuss has to do with business and work. Are we good examples of diligent workers? Does excellence, innovation, and high value define us?

What is business discipline? It comes from leaders who are disciplined: women and men who understand the need for order and integrity, supported by best-in-class competence. When our passion is channeled into processes for ongoing productivity, then we are practicing business discipline.

Solomon offers sound advice about establishing our work before we build our houses and have families. Wise words indeed. Back in the day of small farms, it was prudent to save and pay cash for the land, and then take whatever time and work was required to prepare the fields. Today a young adult is smart to patiently grow in their profession before they pile on responsibilities like marriage, parenting, and debt. It's better for someone to get their financial house in order before purchasing a home. Business discipline sets goals and moves forward by faith.

"God is able to bless you abundantly, so that in all things at all times, having all that you need, you will abound in every good work" (2 Corinthians 9:8).

Fiscal responsibility is an important success factor in business discipline. Project and manage cash flow in a way that provides capital to support ongoing innovation, yet keeps you prepared for an unexpected economic downturn. Staying on or under budget allows a firm to share its profits with the people responsible for its success. Also, fiscal responsibility as a business discipline gives back to the community. God entrusts His abundance to a generous company.

Wise personnel management is a difficult but mission-critical requirement of business discipline. Christian leaders and managers sometimes misinterpret harmony and nonconfrontation as signs of a healthy work culture. However, in almost all growing organizations, some team members who bring them to one stage of growth do not have the giftedness and/or experience to take the enterprise to the next level of success. Loving confrontation regarding a person's limited skill set best serves the employee and the employer. Business discipline involves firing and hiring well. You establish a culture that honors God as you follow a prayerful process of business discipline.

"No discipline seems pleasant at the time, but painful. Later on, however, it produces a harvest of righteousness and peace for those who have been trained by it" (Hebrews 12:11).

Heavenly Father, give me the conviction and courage to manage and lead with a humble business discipline that honors You.

Who on the team do I need to talk with about their need to move into another role?

TAKEAWAY: *Disciplined leaders work in a diligent manner that honors the Lord.*

Consider giving some of these disciplines a try:

1. Take a silent retreat to clearly hear God's voice about matters on your heart.
2. Give your child more time to be a child without rushing to the next activity.
3. Look for ways to apply more personal and professional processes and procedures at work.

Summary of Chapter Six Takeaways

1. Disciplined leaders establish regular routines that grow their devotion to Jesus.
2. Disciplined leaders plant their lives by the water of God's Word, and bear good fruit.
3. Disciplined leaders are wise not to substitute their warm devotion for cold discipline.
4. Disciplined leaders are influenced by other disciplined leaders.
5. Disciplined leaders forgive quickly and remain grateful to God.
6. Disciplined leaders walk with wise leaders, apply their words, and copy their actions.
7. Disciplined leaders learn to listen to the Lord and receive His sweet love.
8. Disciplined leaders are relentless in their pursuit of being still and knowing God.
9. Disciplined leaders take the time to be present and to live in the present.
10. Disciplined leaders work in a diligent manner that honors the Lord.

Chapter Seven

Learning to Lead Like Jesus with Gratitude

*I will never worship anyone but you! For how can I thank
you enough for all you have done? I will surely fulfill my
promises. For my deliverance comes from the Lord alone.*

Jonah 2:9 TLB

*I would maintain that thanks are the highest
form of thought; and that gratitude is
happiness doubled by wonder.*

G.K. Chesterton

Jesus Was Grateful

They took away the stone. Then Jesus looked up and said, 'Father,
I thank you that you have heard me'" (John 11:41).

"Jesus then took the loaves, gave thanks, and distributed to those
who were seated as much as they wanted. He did the same with the
fish" (John 6:11).

Jesus was quick to thank His Father for answered prayer when His
good friend Lazarus was brought back to life. Christ's gratitude gave
glory to God. Jesus also gave thanks for the Lord's incredible provision
when He fed the 5,000. To give thanks to His Father was His honorable response.

My Struggle to Praise God in My Pain

As I recovered from cancer treatment a few years ago, I found the
physical discomfort to be excruciating. I asked my wife, Rita, for the
pain medication. I also asked her to hold me and play the worship
song "How He Loves Us." We sat together, embracing each other as
we praised and worshipped God. A phrase in the song, having to do

with afflictions and God's glory, became very real in my painful condition. In the middle of our little worship service, I felt a great outpouring of my heavenly Father's love. Praising God in my pain released His reassuring refrain, "I love you."

Praise to God is the fruit of gratitude to God, yet sometimes I drift toward self-pity when I stumble and bumble along, trapped in a victim mindset. I strive to be a good follower of my Savior Jesus, yet I fail to live out wisdom in leadership when emotional or physical pain captures my thinking and depletes my energy. Like someone obsessed in their virtual reality headset, I can create my own world devoid of the reality of God's love, forgiveness, and holiness. My self-obsession digs a grave for gratitude and buries it with my chronic busyness. Fortunately, when the pain of my complaining exceeds the pain of my lack of praise to the Lord, the Holy Spirit revives my confused soul. Gratitude and praise to Christ recalibrate the reality of God's control.

> **A Point to Ponder:** Pain positions us to go deeper with loved ones and deeper with the Lord.

In Jonah's case his joyful praise (Jonah 2:9) was the prelude to his expulsion out of the fish's mouth onto dry land. In the darkest hour, we can choose to sing with thankful adoration to our Almighty God. Grateful praise cuts into a lonely soul, embedding hope. With surgeon-like precision, salvation in Jesus removes our deadly tumor of sin and sets free faith's life-giving blood. As anxiety knocks at our heart's door, we drown out its noise by immersing ourselves in praise music.

"Let us come before him with thanksgiving and extol him with music and song" (Psalm 95:2).

Grateful praise gushes forth from a heart full of God. We cannot contain our gratitude to our good and gracious Father. In spite of our flirtation with worthless idols, the Spirit woos us back with His immeasurable love. Our fervent worship of the King who died for us causes an emotional lump in our throats and tears to stream down our cheeks. Grateful praise is a river that forever nourishes the soul. We can't keep quiet because of the loud voice of love that cried out on the cross.

A Point to Ponder: Gratitude and praise to Christ remind us of the reality of God's control.

Our salvation in Jesus takes us into grateful praise that drives back the enemy. Satan cannot stand songs about salvation in Jesus because these biblical, emotional, and harmonious truths are not easily forgotten. We regularly sing of being led away from the delusion of sin into the reality of God's will. Once we were spiritually blind; now the eyes of our soul see Christ, full of love, compassion, and holiness. Grateful praise adorns our spirit with the beauty of God's goodness. Praise Him!

Our uplifting moments of worship to God are His opportunity to remind us of our obligations to Him. When we see Him in all His glory, we envision His call to purity. Pure motives, pure thinking, pure reading, pure watching, pure conversations, pure relationships, pure business dealings, and pure joy all flow from sacrifices of thankfulness offered to our heavenly Father. Similar to Jonah, we offer grateful praise to God in the middle of our tough circumstances and watch Him convert our problems into opportunities. Praise Him!

Wisdom in leadership overcomes pain with persistent praise.

"Sing to the LORD with grateful praise; make music to our God on the harp" (Psalm 147:7).

Heavenly Father, I lift my heart of grateful praise to You in joyful adoration. Show me Your way, so I may walk in Your love.

TAKEAWAY: Grateful leaders look to the Lord often with heartfelt praise and thanksgiving.

Grateful Faith Is Evidence of a Life Healed by God

"'Was no one found who returned to give glory to God, except this foreigner?' And He said to him, 'Stand up and go; your faith has made you well'" (Luke 17:18-19 NASB).

Remember the story of the ten lepers who were healed by Jesus, and only one came back to thank Him? It seems even today, only 10 percent of the population takes the time to return to the Blesser—God—and thank Him for His blessings.

Grateful faith gets to the heart of the matter. It engages God's heart and it heals my heart. Before I met Jesus I was a broken boy, from a broken home, in need of wholeness in my body, soul, and mind. I was spiritually sick and in need of a Savior, but for years I was like the walking dead—unaware of my soul's unhealthy condition. Too busy to pray, I busied myself with school, sports, and social events. But in the middle of a teenage crisis (a car accident) I prayed. I needed to change before I severely hurt myself or someone else. The Lord began the process of healing my broken heart.

Jesus showed mercy to ten sick lepers by healing their disease as they were on their way to meet with the spiritual authorities of their day. Christ knew their physical healing was an opportunity for them to experience God. Desperate to rid themselves of their debilitating disease, these social outcasts obeyed the Lord's command. All ten started by calling on Jesus, but only one (who also suffered from racial rejection) went back to his Savior and Lord to personally thank Him. Those who hurt the most are able to experience a deeper work of grace that compels them to praise God.

"Lord, you are my God; I will exalt you and praise your name, for in perfect faithfulness you have done wonderful things, things planned long ago" (Isaiah 25:1).

A Point to Ponder: Grateful faith leads to ongoing healing of a broken life.

Have you been marginalized because of your race, gender, or religion? Are you in need of spiritual, emotional, or physical wholeness? Your salvation in Christ is only the beginning of His work of grace in your life. Some old habits are transformed in an instant, but others take years to change. Perhaps there are childhood or teenage wounds you ignore; they still thrash around in your soul. If emotions are buried alive, they manifest themselves later in unhealthy expressions. If you have such deep wounds, humble yourself and meet with a good Christian counselor. Grateful faith gets help that facilitates God's healing.

Moreover, be intentional to express grateful faith to God and others. Praise Him for His perfect faithfulness, for His wonderful works, and for the plans He established long ago, just for you. Thank the Lord for healing your heart wounded by sin, sorrow, and death. Grateful faith keeps you from taking for granted God's blessings. The Lord's wholeness in your life gives you the capacity to love and thank others. You are blessed to be a blessing. You are forgiven to forgive. You are accepted to accept others. Your grateful faith qualifies you for wholeness and holiness.

"Giving joyful thanks to the Father, who has qualified you to share in the inheritance of his holy people in the kingdom of light" (Colossians 1:12).

Heavenly Father, grow my grateful faith so I can grow into a healthy Jesus follower.

TAKEAWAY: Grateful leaders have a pattern of ongoing thankfulness to God and people.

Gratitude Flows Freely from a Heart Restored by the Love of Christ

"We will not turn away from you; revive us, and we will call on your name. Restore us, Lord God Almighty; make your face shine on us, that we may be saved" (Psalm 80:18-19).

My wife, Rita, and I grew up in a small town surrounded by 40-acre farms and chicken houses. Maybe some of you can relate! Twenty years into our marriage, Rita happily inherited her grandmother's dining room table, china cabinet, and buffet. Positive emotions flooded her heart at the memory of holidays around these silent accessories to joy and good food. Crispy fried chicken—any leftovers remained on the buffet after lunch for anyone to snack on and even enjoy for dinner. Cornbread was served from a hot cast-iron skillet—handled gingerly with puffy oven mitts—that left its faded mark on the veneered wooden surface. Marks from a carefree childhood were etched all over this rare prize.

We borrowed a pickup truck and made our way on a three-hour adventure from Atlanta to Alabama to collect these neglected antiques and restore them to their original forms. We backed up to a dilapidated shed that had a rusty sheet-metal roof, leaning as if it might collapse at any moment. We brushed back curtains of cobwebs positioned to enmesh our faces, and finally found our treasures, half covered by a dirty blue tarp. We covered the forgotten furniture with moving blankets and bungeed them securely in the back of the truck.

Back home I found a furniture restoration professional who confidently "baptized" (immersed) each wooden piece into a chemical vat, thoroughly stripping away the generational layers of finish. Over the next few weeks he applied cherry wood stain—most soothing to the eyes. With joy, this memory-bearing relic from Rita's childhood was restored and placed in our dining room as a reminder of our need to reach and restore those people, places, and things that need our patient attention and love. Grateful leaders celebrate the all-sufficiency of Christ in their lives and the lives of others.

"Brothers and sisters, if someone is caught in a sin, you who live by the Spirit should restore that person gently. But watch yourselves, or you also may be tempted" (Galatians 6:1).

A Point to Ponder: Grateful leaders are intentional in investing in relationships in need of restoration.

What family member or friend needs you to reach out to them, help them dust away disappointed dreams, and remind them of their hope in Christ's love? To reach out is relationally messy and at times emotionally dirty, but the time, energy, and money invested can produce a beautiful life restored by the grace of God. We reach and God restores. We pray and sometimes we become the Lord's answer to our prayers. We are loved by Christ, so we can love others with His love. Trust Jesus to bring spiritual, emotional, relational, and physical restoration in His perfect timing.

"Restore to me the joy of your salvation and grant me a willing spirit, to sustain me" (Psalm 51:12).

Heavenly Father, give me the courage and care to reach out to others, while trusting You to restore them by Your grace.

TAKEAWAY: Grateful leaders celebrate Christ's restoration of their lives and the lives of others.

A Grateful Nation Gives Thanks to the Lord

"In that day you will say: 'Give thanks to the LORD, call on his name; make known among the nations what he has done, and proclaim that his name is exalted'" (Isaiah 12:4).

Great nations are grateful nations. Our nation is drifting further and further from Christ; we are becoming more distant from the biblical values and principles God originally blessed. Let's remind ourselves what it means to be a nation who often thanks the Lord, not just on Thanksgiving Day!

Will we follow the faith of our nation's founding fathers, or will we cower before the smug elites who delight in criticizing our faith in Christ? It's better to become like our leaders who made America great by their goodness, their gumption, and their love of country, than to feel shamed by those who deride religion as a sham. Our pluralistic society can experience a unified spirit with humility, grateful hearts, respect for one another, and faith in Holy God.

A nation born with religious liberty has much to thank Almighty God for. We can thank Him that man's tyranny lives oceans away and we are free to worship, vote, and treat our fellow citizens with civility and respect. "With your hand you drove out the nations and planted our ancestors; you crushed the peoples and made our ancestors flourish" (Psalm 44:2). God is the initiator and sustainer of our nation's freedom; without the Lord we lose.

A large lump fills our throats when we remember men and women whose blood saturated the soil of foreign fields to preserve our freedoms. The free enterprise, free speech, free press, and free worship of our nation comes with a severe sacrifice. When was the last time you thanked the Lord for those on the front lines who risk their lives for your liberty? His blessing remains where gratitude is retained, so thank Him often.

Indeed, it is a country with character that positions itself for God's blessing. Therefore, don't just ask God to bless America, but also thank Him for already blessing America. "With praise and thanksgiving they sang to the LORD: 'He is good; his love to Israel endures forever'" (Ezra 3:11). A grateful nation gives God the glory for His goodness. Out of our national appreciation the world wonders what God can do for them. So, when the United States of America appreciates Almighty God, we become a shining light as men and women around the globe take notice of our humble dependence on Him.

Jesus described the collective role of God-fearing people: "You are the light of the world. A city on a hill cannot be hidden" (Matthew 5:14).

If we extinguish our light by abandoning the faith from which we came, God will raise up other nations to take our place. However, He smiles when He sees a nation acknowledge Him as Lord and Savior; it leads those who admire our freedoms to look for where they originated. Memorial Day is an opportunity to privately and publicly give God the glory and express gratitude for His incredible favor and blessing on our nation.

"Blessed is the nation whose God is the LORD, the people he chose for his inheritance" (Psalm 33:12).

How can I lead my extended family in a sincere prayer of thanksgiving to the Lord? What are some specific freedoms I can thank God for in blessing my country?

Grateful Leaders Work for the Lord

"Whatever you do, work at it with all your heart, as working for the Lord, not for human masters, since you know that you will receive an inheritance from the Lord as a reward. It is the Lord Christ you are serving" (Colossians 3:23-24).

Work is one of the best places to model an attitude of gratitude. Do your co-workers like to see you coming because of your thankful heart, or do they avoid you because of your demanding disposition?

My precious mother-in-law is a recovering stroke victim. Just last year her sodium dropped to such a low level, she could have easily drifted into a coma. As my wife, Rita, sat by her mom's bedside, a hospital attendant walked in and began joyfully cleaning the room. Rita described to me how this loving person presented an angelic-type encounter.

The attendant worked tirelessly as she meticulously cleaned the hospital room. Every object shone brightly after she rubbed her sanitized cloth over it—the surface of the metal mirror frame, the steel bed support, the mobile meal table—all surfaces that might harbor germs. Rita, recognizing the hospital attendant's energetic work, commented, "Teresa, you must sleep well at night." Sincerely she replied, "I sleep well every night. The Lord gives me good sleep. I work for the Lord. I used to do those drugs and alcohol, but not for seven years. I was rescued, and now I work for the Lord."

Teresa continued, "I worked my way up to this job and am glad I can do good work for all these people who need me. Like your mother—she's going to be okay; she is a good woman. Reminds me of my momma. My momma saw me work here for three years before she passed. Yes, momma saw me work for the Lord and not do those old drugs and alcohol." Rita felt she was in the presence of greatness, a great woman who acknowledged and served her great God. Teresa's gratitude was infectious and her work ethic for her Lord—worshipful!

"Do not work for food that spoils, but for food that endures to eternal life, which the Son of Man will give you. For on him God the Father has placed his seal of approval" (John 6:27).

A Point to Ponder: *Gladness bubbles out effervescently from the hearts of those who work for God.*

What is the motivation behind your work? Are you just working for a paycheck, to put food on the table, furniture in the house, gas in the car, children in the school, and eventually to fund a retirement to spend on yourself? If this is your small, self-focused perspective, there is a much larger and more fulfilling vision out there for you to embrace. The Lord Jesus Christ is the owner of all commerce and economic development. God is in charge of job placement, promotions, and career advancement. The Holy Spirit moves the hearts of decision-makers to make choices that align with the Lord's will. So, work for the Lord's eternal ways.

Always, always be grateful to God for the physical, mental, emotional, and spiritual health He has given you so you can carry out your job responsibilities. Manage yourself and your time as if your Master Jesus might drop by at any moment and inspect your work. What would He find? Diligence or halfheartedness? Excellence or expedience? Counting the minutes or wondering where the time went? Maybe you need a fresh start—a new challenge. Take whatever means necessary, so your work means something. Loving leaders boldly declare, "I work for the Lord!" He gives you purpose. He gives you peace. He is your Master and Lord.

"Why spend money on what is not bread, and your labor on what does not satisfy? Listen, listen to me, and eat what is good, and you will delight in the richest of fare" (Isaiah 55:2).

*Heavenly Father, help me not forget that I
work for You and with You to do great work.*

Where in my work do I need to up my game, to reflect my gratitude to God?

TAKEAWAY: *Grateful leaders who work for the Lord are able to joyfully serve others.*

The Great Joy of Grateful Children

"I have no greater joy than to hear that my children are walking in the truth" (3 John 1:4).

Gratitude is a wonderful gift we can give to our children, and our children can give to us. It brings overwhelming joy to the heart of a parent when they witness an appreciative child. Hearing "Thank you," "You are welcome," and "How can I help?" is music to the ears of a mom and dad who long for their loved ones to grow into grateful adults. Nothing is more disheartening than an ungrateful child. With our children, Rita and I have experienced both the ugliness of ingratitude and the beauty of gratefulness.

The honesty, humility, and purity of a child presents a compelling object lesson. This is very fresh for us as Rita and I absolutely love being "BiBi" and "Pop"—grandmother and grandfather. There are a lot of things in life that are overrated, but being a grandparent is not one of them! When our six-year-old grandson or seven-year-old granddaughter humbly and gratefully say, "Pop, thank you for the pancakes; can I have another one?" I am eager to wait on them and give them more pancakes, along with extra butter and syrup! Their sweet, honest, and humble hearts are as pliable as Play-Doh.

Thankfulness is a vaccine against selfishness and discontent. Children and teenagers who understand and apply appreciation are quick to serve others and not demand their own needs or wants be met. They take to heart what God expects of His sons and daughters: "Do nothing out of selfish ambition or vain conceit. Rather, in humility value others above yourselves, not looking to your own interests but each of you to the interests of the others" (Philippians 2:3-4). Gratitude leads to a Christlike attitude.

So, how can you help your child learn to live a life of thanksgiving and gratitude? What does it take for a teenager to learn to meet the needs of others before addressing their own needs? One thought is to begin early, teaching your child the value of hard work. Assign them chores and pay them when the job is completed with excellence. Then train them to divide their money into the categories of give, save, and spend. When they invest time and energy into a meaningful outcome, they are much more appreciative of the money.

> **A Point to Ponder:** *Seeds of gratitude germinate in a heart of humility and service to others.*

Perhaps you might have them accompany you as you feed the homeless, care for a family in financial distress, or visit those confined to jail. You may decide on a family mission trip overseas. It may be for a construction project, evangelism outreach, or to give love to orphans. Contentment and gratitude will erupt from the heart of your child when they engage people who smile in the face of ugly circumstances. They will see firsthand that joy comes from Jesus, not stuff.

Therefore, be intentional about modeling appreciation in front of your offspring. Be quick to thank God and others, and slow to complain. Grateful children are attractive and pleasant to be around. Their appreciative attitude will serve them well the rest of their lives. Grateful leaders model thankfulness to their family and facilitate a home environment of gratitude.

"In your relationships with one another, have the same mindset as Christ Jesus: Who, being in very nature God, did not consider equality with God something to be used to his own advantage; rather, he made himself nothing by taking the very nature of a servant, being made in human likeness. And being found in appearance as a man, he humbled himself by becoming obedient to death—even death on a cross!" (Philippians 2:5-8).

How can I model an attitude of gratitude in front of my children? What can we do as a family to learn appreciation and experience contentment?

> **TAKEAWAY:** *Grateful leaders facilitate home environments of gratitude for their families.*

A grateful heart is like maple syrup over a waffle: Everything it touches tastes better. Make it a goal to thank God every day. Perhaps you could start a gratitude journal so you don't forget God's blessings! "Praise the LORD, my soul, and forget not all his benefits" (Psalm 103:2).

David's prayer of gratitude to God:

> Yours is the mighty power and glory and victory and majesty. Everything in the heavens and earth is yours, O Lord, and this is your kingdom. We adore you as being in control of everything. Riches and honor come from you alone, and you are the ruler of all mankind; your hand controls power and might, and it is at your discretion that men are made great and given strength. O our God, we thank you and praise your glorious name (1 Chronicles 29:11-13 TLB).

What prayer of gratitude is the Lord asking you to pray? What praise song is He asking you to sing? Your gratitude gives you an attractive attitude.

Summary of Chapter Seven Takeaways

1. Grateful leaders look to the Lord often with heartfelt praise and thanksgiving.

2. Grateful leaders have a pattern of ongoing thankfulness to God and people.

3. Grateful leaders celebrate Christ's restoration of their lives and the lives of others.

4. Grateful leaders are thankful to God for a nation where we can enjoy the benefits of freedom.

5. Grateful leaders who work for the Lord are able to joyfully serve others.

6. Grateful leaders facilitate home environments of gratitude for their families.

Chapter Eight

Learning to Lead Like Jesus with Generosity

A generous person will prosper;
whoever refreshes others will be refreshed.

Proverbs 11:25

It is better to return a borrowed pot with a
little something you last cooked in it.

An Omaha (Native American) Proverb

Jesus Was Generous

Very truly I tell you, whoever believes in me will do the works I have been doing, and they will do even greater things than these, because I am going to the Father. And I will do whatever you ask in my name, so that the Father may be glorified in the Son. You may ask me for anything in my name, and I will do it" (John 14:12-14).

Jesus was generous with His power and influence. He informed the disciples and all who would believe that they would do even greater works than He had accomplished. When the Lord Christ ascended to heaven, the Holy Spirit descended to empower and equip followers of Jesus. Greater works were immediately experienced, with thousands at Pentecost from all tongues and tribes receiving God's grace through faith in Christ. Today Jesus's gift is still giving in transformed lives. Christianity has a global impact on churches, hospitals, schools, businesses, and governments.

A Generous Leader Who Stepped Out in Faith

I met Barbara over 15 years ago and immediately was impressed with her passion to help people, and her love for Christ. The non-profit she has led the past 30-plus years is North Fulton Community

Charities, in Roswell, Georgia. Their mission: "To build self-sufficiency and prevent homelessness and hunger in our community by providing emergency assistance and enrichment programs." NFCC is a leader in North Fulton, offering assistance to over 5,000 families annually. Last year, food was distributed over 20,000 times; over 2,000 families utilized clothing vouchers; and $1.3 million was expended for direct aid to clients in need of financial assistance. Families representing 18,000 people have received financial assistance, access to a food pantry and a thriving thrift store, family training, and Thanksgiving/ Christmas assistance. Their Education Center offers an array of classes and opportunities to help residents move toward financial stability and self-sufficiency. An organization with such a wide variety of services and expansive influence in the community requires an equally diverse group of gifted volunteers and staff.[10]

Here is Barbara's story in her own words:

> My family moved to Atlanta in 1978. I was then a stay-at-home mom with four kids, all born in different states. International Harvester transferred us, and it was my pattern to try to get involved in the community as quickly as possible. We lived in a neighborhood where everybody was pretty much like us, all young families raising children. I went looking for something that would allow me to interact with people of different ages and ethnicities.
>
> I'd grown up in a multi-ethnic neighborhood in a suburb of Boston, so it just didn't seem real to me for everybody to be the same. Of course, with young children, most of our interaction was with the parents of our kids' friends. I literally was looking for something that did not involve my children and that put me in touch with real life.
>
> Soon I found what was then called "The Clothes Closet," that my church and a number of other churches had started a few years before. Our church's day to volunteer was Friday, so I jumped in and quickly became the

chairperson. If the Clothes Closet had any money left over at the end of the month, we would write a check to charities.

Surprisingly we became one of the bigger donors to charities! After a couple of years the board decided maybe we should have staff, and it was at the perfect moment in my life, so I said, "Can I apply?" I was hired as the executive director!

Instead of coasting, Barbara engaged life by following God's call!

TAKEAWAY: *Generous leaders invest their time and expertise to serve a diverse range of people.*

Generous Women Who Supported Jesus

"Also some women who had been cured of evil spirits and diseases: Mary (called Magdalene) from whom seven demons had come out; Joanna the wife of Chuza, the manager of Herod's household; Susanna; and many others. These women were helping to support them [Jesus and His 12 disciples] out of their own means" (Luke 8:2-3).

Women who were ministered to by Jesus were His first supporters.

My wife, Rita, is the most generous woman I know. She gives abundantly of her time. Rita meets with younger moms and wives who desperately need encouragement and tools to navigate a very demanding season of life. She loves to systematically give donations to our church and ministries on the front lines of faith for Christ. Every month it brings me joy to watch her gratefully celebrate God's work by reading every word, of every newsletter, for every ministry we support. Rita's capacity to give is a model I aspire to follow. Her generosity is joyfully infectious.

Mary, Joanna, Susanna, and others helped support Jesus and the disciples out of their own means. Why? One compelling reason was Christ had changed their lives. He freed Mary from the insidious influence of seven demons. Perhaps Joanna and Susanna were exceedingly grateful to Jesus for healing a family member or forgiving a friend of her sins. These women gave to Jesus because they were grateful to Him. Not only did they give financially, but they gave by being with Him. Watching Him care for people's needs, they rolled up their sleeves and served alongside.

> **A Point to Ponder:** *A heart touched by Jesus is compelled to serve and give in His name.*

"In the midst of a very severe trial, their overflowing joy and their extreme poverty welled up in rich generosity. For I testify that they gave as much as they were able, and even beyond their ability" (2 Corinthians 8:2-3).

You may be in a season of life where you feel limited in your ability to give. You may even find yourself in a situation where you need to be more on the receiving end. Your heavenly Father understands your capacity to give, but make sure you don't allow your circumstances to define your richness. The magnitude of a gift is not defined by size, but by capacity. When you give as much as you are able to give, you support the Lord's work, and He will do a deeper work in your life!

We start by giving all of ourselves to our Savior Jesus. A life 100 percent invested in the kingdom of God enjoys an abundant return on investment in what matters most now and into eternity. Our generosity is not necessarily defined by larger gifts, but by our larger love for our heavenly Father. A life of love is compelled to give—even beyond our ability. Yes, we are wise to surround ourselves with other generous givers so we can celebrate what Christ is doing. Generous loving leads to generous giving. Generous women (and men) find great fulfillment!

"They urgently pleaded with us for the privilege of sharing in this service to the Lord's people. And they exceeded our expectations: They gave themselves first of all to the Lord, and then by the will of God also to us" (2 Corinthians 8:4-5).

Heavenly Father, give me a heart of generosity
so I am able to give generously.

TAKEAWAY: *Generous leaders give out of gratitude for what God has given.*

Renewing and Restoring a Community by Generous Giving

Jess and Angela Correll, seventh-generation Kentuckians, are not your momma and daddy's bankers. They are small-town citizens who transformed their community by aggressively investing in the abilities and potential of others. By God's grace they own community banks across Kentucky, a life insurance company, a restaurant, a soap store, guesthouses, farms, and far too many investments in God's kingdom to mention.

I admire Jess and Angela, because instead of trying to do everything themselves, they resource trusted leaders to carry their particular God-called mission. Angela is also the successful author of two novels and is working on a third. They are wise leaders worth following, who invest in dozens of other wise leaders worth following!

Here is the abridged version of an interview I hosted with Jess and Angela:

> *Boyd:* Talk about the vision the Lord gave you for the three pillars you use as a prayerful guide on how to invest in others.
>
> *Angela:* We talk about three pillars because that's how we've distilled our vision: excellence, stewardship, and hospitality.

1. Excellence

> *Jess/Angela:* With excellence we don't mean being perfect, because we can't be perfect in this world; we're imperfect people. But we can strive for excellence, and we need to strive for excellence because we want to reflect God. Really anything less than our absolute best is not a good reflection of Him. And so, we want to do our best to be

excellent in everything we do, from the way guests experience our businesses, to the quality of our products, to our hotel accommodations and guesthouses, to the restaurant's personalized service and appetizing food. We work and pray toward all of our initiatives being supported by the excellence pillar.

A Point to Ponder: Excellent work can be a catalyst to support generous initiatives.

2. Stewardship

"Each of you should use whatever gift you have received to serve others, as faithful stewards of God's grace in its various forms" (1 Peter 4:10).

Jess/Angela: Stewardship is not only about our finances, but also about stewarding our old buildings, because preserving them reminds us of our rich heritage. It is actually honoring the people that worked on them originally—100 years ago—the labor and the sweat, all the creative aspects of how the buildings were built. We're valuing their legacy, stewarding that labor, and trying to manage it well. Stewardship is also caring for our bodies through the highest quality food. And then again the food really goes into stewarding the planet (God's creation), because sustainable farming is providing food for the community that is wholesome, healthy, and local.

And then even in the store with our goat milk products, again, it's a stewardship of the animals, the land, and our bodies with products like soap, lotion, and shaving cream. They have no harmful preservatives linked to diseases; we try to avoid anything undesirable or unfit. So holistic stewardship focuses on a lot of levels: money, historic preservation, time, products, services, personnel, food, animals, and the environment.

> **A Point to Ponder:** *Wise management of resources creates a margin for generosity.*

3. Hospitality

"They have gone out to serve under the banner of the Name, and they do not accept gifts from those outside our faith community. We should give people like this our full support so that we can share in this work for the truth" (3 John 1:7-8 THE VOICE).

Jess/Angela: Hospitality cuts across all three of the businesses, including the bank, but I'm primarily talking about the downtown Stanford, Kentucky, businesses. The warm welcome you're greeted with when you walk in makes you feel at home and makes you feel relaxed and comfortable. We want people to feel loved and refreshed. When they come and stay at the guesthouses, we want their blood pressure to go down and their joy to go up. When visitors drive into Stanford, we want them to relax, to feel like they are at home. And then hopefully when they leave, to take all of that with them and make the part of the world where they live a better place.

> **A Point to Ponder:** *Hospitality may be the most practical, helpful way to give to others.*

"You may say to yourself, 'My power and the strength of my hands have produced this wealth for me.' But remember the LORD your God, for it is he who gives you the ability to produce wealth, and so confirms his covenant, which he swore to your ancestors, as it is today" (Deuteronomy 8:17-18).

Boyd: What motivates your generosity and trust in others? What's one story that comes to mind that gave you great joy from being generous?

Angela: Honestly, generosity just really makes us happy. And I know that's such a simple, simple response, but there really isn't anything more complicated to it than that. It makes us happy and we feel blessed when we are able to give, and we've also had to learn to receive at times. Sometimes for a giver it's awfully hard to receive, and I've had to learn that if I don't receive from other people, then I'm denying them that blessing.

But I think it just makes us happy. It warms our heart. We feel like the distance runner, Eric Liddell, who, after the 1928 Olympics, said that he felt God's pleasure when he ran. He did not run on Sunday, but ran a different race on another day and won! And I think that's a little bit of how we feel when we give. We just feel God's pleasure in being generous.

Jess: Life is just so much more fun when you're giving. Life can become a little bit of a hurricane or tornado, and it's a joy to be able to log into our National Christian Foundation account on Sunday afternoon and give money to organizations or individuals in real need. But really, we give more money to people. The school that you were on the board of, Boyd, Good Samaritans (we always say "that school in Delhi, India, for slum kids"), is our second home. Instead of another residence, with upkeep, headaches, and taxes to pay—that beautiful Christian school for the poor is more fulfilling and needed than a beach house for the rich.

A Point to Ponder: *Spirit-led spontaneous giving leads to fulfillment for the giver and receiver.*

Jess/Angela: Also, we have dear friends of ours—a husband and wife who do "spontaneous giving" (non-tax deductible)—they just give from their own giving fund, and they can give up to $1,000 to these things out of a personal checking account without consulting with each other. Our friends said it was for people who had lost their jobs or were sick, maybe with cancer. I think maybe if their own house was getting foreclosed on they would still help with someone else's house payment or rent!

And what I really love about the spontaneous approach to generosity is that you have to be paying attention, because if you're thinking about your own agenda all the time, these opportunities will come and go and you'll miss them. "What did you say? What did you need?" I've had the most wonderful things happen, people who could not believe it, just so thankful, and I've had people say, "I'm in great shape financially and I don't need any help. Just give that to the next person." What does the Bible say? A generous life is a life that's truly life (1 Timothy 6:19).

You'll never regret any of the things you give away. You might regret buying something, but I can't think of one thing we look back on and say we regret having given it to somebody.

Angela: Even if we found out later it was misused, we just feel like that's between them and the Lord.

Jess: I'd rather be on radical generosity's side than to be closed-handed.

Boyd: Yes, as Billy Graham said years ago, as long as we keep an open hand, God will entrust us with more we can give away. Thanks, Jess and Angela, for inspiring us all in not just generous giving, but also in generous living!

> **TAKEAWAY:** Generous leaders invest in their communities economically and spiritually.

How the Monkeys Saved the Fish

Thinking about my interview with these generosity giants, I was reminded of the traditional Tanzanian folktale "The Monkey and the Fish." This is a creative reminder of the need to really understand how to help others in a way they need to be helped, and how we are to patiently listen and learn.

> The rainy season that year had been the strongest ever and the river had broken its banks. There were floods everywhere and the animals were all running up into the hills. The floods came so fast that many drowned, except the lucky monkeys who used their agility to climb up into the treetops. They looked down on the surface of the water where the fish were swimming and gracefully jumping out of the water as if they were the only ones enjoying the devastating flood.
>
> One of the monkeys saw the fish and shouted to his companion: "Look down, my friend, look at those poor creatures. They are going to drown. Do you see how they struggle in the water?" "Yes," said the other monkey. "What a pity! Probably they were late in escaping to the hills because they seem to have no legs. How can we save them?" "I think we must do something. Let's go close to the edge of the flood where the water is not deep enough to cover us, and we can help them to get out."
>
> So the monkeys did just that. They started catching the fish, but not without difficulty. One by one, they

brought them out of the water and put them carefully on the dry land. After a short time there was a pile of fish lying on the grass motionless. One of the monkeys said, "Do you see? They were tired, but now they are just sleeping and resting. Had it not been for us, my friend, all these poor creatures without legs would have drowned."

The other monkey said: "They were trying to escape from us because they could not understand our good intentions. But when they wake up they will be very grateful because we have brought them salvation."[11]

Wow, a creative reminder of when our helping can hurt, and the need to humbly learn how to help someone in a healthy manner!

Our Creatively Generous Heavenly Father

"Let them give thanks to the LORD for his unfailing love and his wonderful deeds for mankind, for he satisfies the thirsty and fills the hungry with good things" (Psalm 107:8-9).

What is behind our heavenly Father's giving heart? I'm so glad God's essence is generosity, in how He gave the gift of His only Son Jesus, what we needed most. What a creative, generous, and loving Lord we serve!

This story from my friend Brian Kluth is a touching illustration of the Lord's generous provision for a single parent:

Nancy was a single mother with young children. Her ex-husband sent her only a small amount of grocery money every week, so small it couldn't even feed one person, much less her family of four. But Nancy decided to begin giving to God from her little bit of grocery money and trust Him to provide. Shortly after, she got a job with a cookbook company. The company paid Nancy to go grocery shopping and prepare meals so they could take photographs for their cookbooks. When they were done taking pictures, Nancy could keep the food she had purchased and prepared. Isn't that an amazing story of God's goodness? Nancy learned that even if you're poor, you still need to learn to give from whatever you have.[12]

The generosity of our God is unprecedented, with His unfailing love and His wonderful deeds. He gives rest when we are weary. He gives peace when we are fearful. He gives joy when we are sad. He gives comfort when we are sorrowful. He gives forgiveness when we are guilty. He gives hope when we are doubtful. He gives us His Son Jesus for salvation, and His Holy Spirit for our comfort, conviction, and direction. He gives!

Why is the Lord so extremely charitable to His children? He gives because He loves. He loves you too much to leave you lost in your sins. This is why He gave Jesus as your gift, for forgiveness. He loves you too much to leave you bound by lies. This is why He gave you the Holy Spirit, to lead you in all truth. The revelation and understanding of truth is part of the Lord's abundant provision and freedom to live well.

"He who forms the mountains, who creates the wind, and who reveals his thoughts to mankind" (Amos 4:13).

A Point to Ponder: God's radical generosity supplies His children with an excess of grace to live well, and an abundance of gifts to serve well.

God gives you contentment in your work, and wealth and possessions to enjoy. "When God gives someone wealth and possessions, and the ability to enjoy them, to accept their lot and be happy in their toil—this is a gift of God" (Ecclesiastes 5:19). Thank Him for what you have and trust Him for what you don't have.

Since God has been so generous to you, how can you now be generous to others? Perhaps you can give grace instead of judgment, forgiveness instead of resentment, transparency instead of deception, and freedom instead of control. Do you have family or friends that desperately need you to listen, offer advice, and provide financial assistance?

Pray for God's provision for people you know, and then be available as an answer to your own prayers.

"I pray that out of his glorious riches he may strengthen you with power through his Spirit in your inner being, so that Christ may dwell in your hearts through faith. And I pray that you, being rooted and established in love…" (Ephesians 3:16-17).

Am I grateful to God for His goodness and gifts to me? To whom can I offer generosity in Jesus's name?

TAKEAWAY: *Generous leaders are called to generous living by the radical, generous love of God.*

As our pastor says, "Give giving a try and see what happens." I agree, but don't limit your generosity to money. Cash is just the beginning. Take an inventory of your relationships, expertise, experiences, assets, and time, and pray about creative ways to invest them in God's kingdom!

Summary of Chapter Eight Takeaways

1. Generous leaders invest their time and expertise to serve a diverse range of people.

2. Generous leaders give out of gratitude for what God has given.

3. Generous leaders invest in their communities economically and spiritually.

4. Generous leaders are called to generous living by the radical, generous love of God.

Chapter Nine

Learning to Lead Like Jesus with Forgiveness

*Be kind and compassionate to one
another, forgiving each other,
just as in Christ God forgave you.*

Ephesians 4:32

*Resentment is like drinking poison and
then hoping it will kill your enemies.*

Unknown Source

Jesus Was Forgiving

When they had come to the place called Calvary, there they crucified Him, and the criminals, one on the right hand and the other on the left. Then Jesus said, 'Father, forgive them, for they do not know what they do'" (Luke 23:33-34 NKJV).

A world ignorant of Christ's love was forgiven by the most powerful person on the planet. Jesus withheld His power of judgment so those blind to His love could receive the power of His forgiveness. In His most dire moment, He had the most compassion and love for others. One perfect man forgave the injustice inflicted on Him, knowing His forgiveness would bring justification to imperfect mankind, if they would trust in Him. Jesus forgave ignorance and offered intimacy with Him in exchange!

What Is Forgiveness?

This is a helpful definition that aligns with a biblical worldview: "Forgiveness is a conscious, deliberate decision to release feelings of resentment or vengeance toward a person or group who has harmed you, regardless of whether they actually deserve your forgiveness.

Forgiveness does not mean forgetting, nor does it mean condoning or excusing offenses."[13]

What Happens When Empty Nesters Need New Skills?

When Rita and I became empty nesters a few years back, we felt the need for a new set of skills, for training to help us better do life together as we anticipated our best years ahead. When our fourth and last daughter moved out to attend college, Rita wept tears of grief, and I wept tears of joy. She missed her baby, and I celebrated that our young adult was almost off the payroll!

We experienced different, sometimes vastly different, ideas of how we felt about our new season of life. One sad, one happy, and both wondering how to spend our time and money. Do we invest primarily in our newly married children and our grandchildren? Or, for what seemed like the first time in our marriage, do something just for ourselves? Being married at 19 meant a very brief single adult life, so how should we feather our empty nest? We needed help to process through each other's expectations.

About the same time we were pondering these investment questions, our friends Bill and Alison visited our home with youthful exuberance about a marriage event they had just attended. Their enthusiasm was infectious. They bubbled over about the communication skills they had acquired. They had begun to use them, with joyful, though sometimes stressful, effectiveness.

They shared with us terminology, like the "emotional cup," and how to fill it with good feelings (forgiveness, joy, contentment, love, romance, hope), and how to process bad feelings (hurt, anger, guilt, fear, false guilt, condemnation, stress). They shared ideas, like how to mourn together and comfort one another before delivering solutions and truth. They shared warnings like: Do not manipulate by being a selfish taker, self-reliant, or self-condemning. Bill and Alison insisted we also invest in this four-day transformational marriage intensive.

Real friends take the time to explain the benefits of shared real-life experiences. Who in your life looks out for your best?

A Point to Ponder: Forgiving leaders resource others to grow in forgiveness.

Four Days of Emotional Exposure

So, we decided to attend, though I didn't want to be emotionally naked in front of anyone, especially strangers. Gradually I undressed my feelings to a scary level of vulnerability, cautiously letting down my guard and inviting God's peace to guard my heart. We showed up on a Sunday afternoon on the campus of Berry College in Rome, Georgia, about 90 miles northwest of Atlanta. The Normandy Inn was designed with the quaint French town in mind, with red ceramic shingles and roughly hewn brown stone exterior. It was a romantic throwback to a genteel European setting.

Our hosts greeted us with a warmth the Ritz Carlton would be envious of, as they directed Rita and me to our beautifully decorated bedroom, with a tall poster bed surrounded by walls with soft colors and soothing art. Interestingly, there were two connected bedrooms, just in case a couple needed some space from each other, or perhaps one suffered from sleep apnea or snoring!

The food and service were both five-star. The excellent meals highlighted freshly prepared Southern cuisine, and those who waited on us had all experienced a marriage intensive like we were attending. They were satisfied customers who wanted to generously serve and invest by volunteering their time and smiles. I can't think of a better endorsement than to give back, because these servers were so impacted by the transformation of their lives. So, together with three other couples—strangers and fellow strugglers, but desiring more—Rita and I began our four-day walk of faith: real, painful, healing, and never boring!

A Point to Ponder: A safe environment of no condemnation invites understanding and empathy.

Our trained Christian PhD counselor was a master at moving all eight of us through a process of unpacking our past and present pain through a genogram exercise. That is a detailed family tree diagram that exposes relational dynamics and dysfunctions. Over the course of two days, each of us diagrammed on a whiteboard our first- and second-removed family trees, describing hurtful relationships and healthy ones. The compelling visual gave me a fresh and vivid understanding of how my heart still had areas of pain in need of comfort and healing. Remarkably, as we began to empathize and engage with our new friends, we were all able to extend comfort and love through verbal understanding, acceptance, and authentic affirmation.

Not surprisingly, my heart for Rita grew fonder as I saw more clearly her incredible capacity to care and nurture, but at the same time her need for being known and to know me. Also, she was able to see my need for approval and acceptance, in a way that brought out the best in me and gave me confidence to lead her and our family well.

Past Hurt Converted into Present Healing

Most importantly, on the last day we experienced a process of authentic confession, repentance, and forgiveness of sin. It revealed a past financial decision I made without Rita's input that hurt her deeply, damaging her trust in me. I thought we had dealt with the pain of my pride and greed, but I discovered Rita's resentment still simmered under the surface of our relationship.

By God's grace, with vulnerability and humility, I used my newly discovered vocabulary about clearly defined sin, looked her in the eyes, asked her forgiveness, and committed to not repeating this mistake in the future. Then from her heart she truly forgave me. The Holy Spirit mended our fractured trust and made us whole again.

A Point to Ponder: Acquired skills of confession and repentance invite forgiveness and healing.

We learned new skills of true confession, repentance, and forgiveness. It was like a child learning to ride a bicycle after removing the training wheels. Since then we have stumbled and stuttered our way through, but we continually improve at resolving issues, sooner rather than later. Our communication is guided by the desire we each have to know how the other feels, and what they need in the moment.

Our other-centered focus keeps us off the crazy cycle where I would go into silent mode with a quiet anger, or Rita's insecurities would feed her fears and distrust. Learning to communicate well takes practice and persistence, but it pays off with relational fruit that feeds our emotions, our minds, and our souls! Wisdom in leadership works toward healing bruised and broken relationships.

TAKEAWAY: *Forgiving leaders engage in the process of confession, repentance, and forgiveness.*

A Forgiving Leader Is Quick to Ask Forgiveness

"I assure you and most solemnly say to you, unless you repent [that is, change your inner self—your old way of thinking, live changed lives] and become like children [trusting, humble, and forgiving], you will never enter the kingdom of heaven. Therefore, whoever humbles himself like this child is greatest in the kingdom of heaven" (Matthew 18:3-4 AMP).

Jesus set the table for forgiveness by defining a precondition for forgiveness: humility. Children are capable of quick forgiveness because they easily allow love and humility to mold their lives. Humility precedes forgiveness.

Recently, I made my way to our neighborhood playground with three grandsons, Hudson (6), Harrison (4), and Marshall (2), in the backseat of my car. Because it is a two-minute drive, I placed all three grandsons in their car seats without buckling them in securely. Hudson, the compliant rule follower, called me out: "Pop, Harrison and Marshall are not strapped in." He, of course, secured himself.

"No worries, we will be there in a jiffy," I quipped. Not the right answer. "No, Pop, they have to be buckled; it's not safe"—and he could have added, "it's against the law!" I tried to ignore his innocent imploring, but he began crying. "Pop, it's not safe! Pop, it's not safe!" Like a balloon with a tiny hole, my pride began to deflate, and my heart began to hurt for this humble little one.

The second I pulled into the playground I hugged Hudson, apologized for not being safe, and asked him and his brothers to forgive me. "I forgive you, Pop; I was just scared." Wow, his humility moved my heart more than the sermons I've heard preached on the topic. Humility prepares all hearts for forgiveness.

TAKEAWAY: *Forgiving leaders embrace humility as a precondition for forgiveness.*

A Forgiving Leader May Need to Extend Ongoing Forgiveness

I struggled with forgiving my dad. It was an ongoing process for a lot of years, but by God's grace, I made progress. He and Mom divorced when I was five, so I have little remembrance of my father from when I was a young child. To be a single parent in 1965 was the exception, and exceptionally hard. Mom detested Dad for some reasons I understood, and to this day, some reasons I still don't. One very painful, practical point of neglect was his failure to pay child support: $50 a month for me and $50 for my brother. I felt abandoned, hurt, angry, and insecure. I began to detest my dad for not being my dad. My heart grew bitter.

My soul stewed in self-pity, while I used busyness to mask my anger, channeling my self-reliant energy into sports, academics, work, and girls. Sound familiar? Maybe you suffer from an adult version of my teenage days. Thankfully, in the spring of my freshman year in college, the Holy Spirit ambushed my spirit with the grace and love of the Lord.

Rita and I had started dating, and her father required me to attend church with them—great dad preparation for our eventual family of four daughters! I reasoned, "I have a business, so I need to know how to conduct business with church people, and she's cute." With no apparent downside, I began to regularly attend church for the first time.

One Sunday the minister talked of the joy of having a heavenly

Father, even if one didn't have an earthly father. In that moment God's love poured over me like warm, liquid chocolate over cake and ice cream. My heart began to melt. Grace captured my affections with comforting images of true love. A few weeks later the pastor lovingly, but urgently, taught on hell. I learned, "The fear of the LORD is the beginning of wisdom" (Proverbs 9:10).

When I went forward to receive Christ at the end of that evening service, Brother Taylor took me by the hand and assured me by saying, "Boyd, I will lead you in a prayer to repent of your sins and trust Jesus Christ as your Lord and Savior." He continued, "You will kneel down a sinner and stand up a saint!" I did, and by faith in Jesus I was no longer a slave to sin and fear—I was truly set free!

Tom, a local businessman, discipled me and my two friends over the next two years. Weekly we studied the Scriptures, prayed together, and shared our faith with our friends. A few months into our Bible study I read what became for me a life-defining verse:

"Forgiving each other, just as in Christ God forgave you" (Ephesians 4:32).

Immediately, I wrote out a prayer and began praying fervently and faithfully: "Forgiving my dad, just as Christ forgave me." Asking, "Lord what does my forgiveness look like in my relationship with my father?" To reinforce this idea, I later learned Jesus's instruction to Peter on forgiveness: Forgive often, and practice ongoing forgiveness—forgive seventy times seven times!

A Point to Ponder: *Forgiveness starts by first receiving Christ's forgiveness of our sins.*

In 1982, after college, I was off to seminary in Fort Worth, Texas, where the largest theological graduate school and the largest honky-tonk were located—and providentially, at that time, the home of General Dynamics's aircraft production division. By "coincidence" my dad was hired as a General Dynamics contractor, working as a technical writer for operational manuals of new military planes. I felt proud of my father's vocation. How cool that he was entrusted with documenting and detailing these projects that supported our national security. I looked forward to growing our relationship.

Over the course of three years, almost every Wednesday night, on the way to prayer service at our church, Rita, little Rebekah, and I would drop by to see Dad and Pat, my stepmom. I didn't really know Dad, and he didn't really know me. Yet like two preschoolers trying to assemble a bicycle, we attempted to build a relationship. Awkward? Yes. Sometimes after 15 minutes of conversation about the weather, and Dad complaining of some government scandal, he would suggest, "Isn't it about time for you to head over to your church?"

One Wednesday night after a rough time with Dad—having endured his cigarette smoke, drinking, and cussing—Rita lamented, "Why do we keep going to his house? He is so mean to you." Determined, I replied, "We know better and he doesn't; we will keep loving him to Jesus." Now, my heart was not always in that place of grace, but she caught me at a good time!

So, I'll conclude by saying, I spent 20 years pursuing my prodigal father—forgiving, crying, screaming along the way. Gratefully, hundreds of believers prayed for Christ to heal George Bailey's heart and our relationship—and He did! Forgiveness is hard, but not forgiving is harder.

TAKEAWAY: *Forgiving leaders have abundant forgiveness even for those who hurt them the most.*

Our Heavenly Father's Ongoing Forgiveness

"Then Peter came to him and asked, 'Lord, how often should I forgive someone who sins against me? Seven times?' 'No, not seven times,' Jesus replied, 'but seventy times seven'" (Matthew 18:21-22 NLT).

"The Kingdom of Heaven can be compared to a king who decided to bring his accounts up to date. In the process, one of his debtors was brought in who owed him $10 million!, literally, '10,000 talents.' He couldn't pay, so the king ordered him sold for the debt, also his wife and children and everything he had. But the man fell down before the king, his face in the dust, and said, 'Oh, sir, be patient with me and I will pay it all.' Then the king was filled with pity for him and released him and forgave his debt" (Matthew 18:23-27 TLB).

Just before Jesus's story about the king's gracious forgiveness of his servant, He answered Peter's inquiry of our long-term obligation or opportunity to forgive another. Jesus scrambled Peter's theological categories by raising the standard of forgiveness to an ongoing process of grace, mercy, and love. In other words, Jesus taught Peter to forgive others as our heavenly Father has forgiven us: all of our sin—past, present, and future!

What a riveting story. Imagine Jesus's audience all leaning forward, just like people at a present-day, gripping movie that draws in its viewers. This was not a time to go to the restroom or buy popcorn! The king, who represents God, is approached by one of his humble servants, who is overwhelmed by his massive debt. This contrite debtor pleads for mercy, as in his culture he would have been assigned to debtors' prison, which would seal his fate: he'd be unable to work and thus pay back his obligations. He would also lose his wife and children, who would be sold to pay down the costly debt.

Fortunately, the servant must have found the king in a good mood, as his master extended mercy by wiping clean the slate of the debtor's unpayable financial obligation. Can you imagine the relief, the emotional eruption of thanksgiving and praise to God? No smelly dungeon, infested with rats and roaches. Instead of cold and darkness—warmth and light. Instead of separation from loved ones—a united home of love, gratitude, and contentment. He was set free by grace and mercy.

TAKEAWAY: *Forgiving leaders are chronically grateful for ongoing forgiveness from God.*

The Torment of Unforgiveness

"When the man left the king, he went to a man who owed him $2,000 and grabbed him by the throat and demanded instant payment.

The man fell down before him and begged him to give him a little time. 'Be patient and I will pay it,' he pled. But his creditor wouldn't wait. He had the man arrested and jailed until the debt would be paid in full. Then the man's friends went to the king and told him what had happened. And the king called before him the man he had forgiven and said, 'You evil-hearted wretch! Here I forgave you all that tremendous debt, just because you asked me to—shouldn't you have mercy on others, just as I had mercy on you?' Then the angry king sent the man to the torture chamber until he had paid every last penny due. So shall my heavenly Father do to you if you refuse to truly forgive your brothers" (Matthew 18:28-35 TLB).

The newly forgiven servant miserably failed to treat his own debtor with the same kind of goodness and grace that had been extended to him, on a much larger scale. With greed the creditor sought out his debtor, violently grabbed his throat, and demanded payment. How could he? Was this a sick joke? No, the forgiven man dismissed his recent grace experience. Why? I don't know for sure. Maybe he felt entitled, or was simply ungrateful. Whatever the reason for his unreasonable recourse, his unruly actions cost him his freedom and his peace. Since the man who was forgiven much failed to forgive much, he was sent to torment.

TAKEAWAY: *Forgiving leaders forgive others to the extent they have been forgiven by Christ.*

God's Conditional Forgiveness

"If you refuse to forgive others, your Father will not forgive your sins" (Matthew 6:15).

"Wait," you may ask, "I thought God's forgiveness is unconditional?" You are right. In Christ forgiveness of sin, salvation, and eternal life in heaven is secured by His sacrificial death and our faith in Him. The other side of the coin of Christ's unconditional forgiveness for heaven is His conditional forgiveness on earth, that allows us to enjoy fellowship with Him and peace with people. Just as the unforgiving servant was sent to the torture chamber, so our souls will live in torment if we choose not to forgive. The absence of peace and rest is the fruit of unforgiveness.

Imagine a pile of bricks, with each brick representing an opportunity to forgive someone. If we choose not to forgive, then each time we sin we add a brick to a wall that blocks our forgiveness from God. Years of not forgiving and sinning builds a high, wide brick wall of isolation, leaving us separated from Christ's cleansing and estranged from the Lord's love. Fortunately, the wall can be removed, brick by brick, as we forgive others—which also then opens the way for Christ's grace, love, and healing.

TAKEAWAY: *Forgiving leaders freely forgive others, and enjoy forgiveness from their Lord Jesus.*

Our Ongoing Forgiveness of Others and Our Freedom

"Then the king was filled with pity for him and released him and forgave his debt" (Matthew 18:27 TLB).

When someone withholds something, I feel anxious. They might withhold an apology, a compliment, an answer to my question, or a reply to my email or text. Disappointment brings an angry reaction to the edge of my lips, and my thoughts obsess over what I feel I should get that is not coming. Yet Jesus described a powerful king who rose above petty, self-focused emotions and, with the respect royalty should show, he cared for a commoner. The monarch extended compassion, freedom, and forgiveness to an undeserving debtor. He had reason to punish, but he forgave instead.

Why should we offer compassion instead of getting even? Freedom instead of bondage? Keeping no record of wrongs instead of holding against our offender a list of hurts? Because our heavenly Father calls us to forgive as He has forgiven us: fully and forever. If we don't forgive, we choose to be controlled by the actions of someone we can't control. To not forgive ignores a melanoma of mind, body, and emotions.

Resentment, like a cancer, eats away our joy and starves our peace. Wisdom in leadership leans into forgiveness, to bring healing to our relational health.

Compassion looks a person in the eye and wonders what they have experienced. Maybe they lashed out in anger because they were the brunt of another's bitterness. Were they ever abused? Abandoned? Lost? Hurt? Rejected? Forgotten? Perhaps they suffered great loss from the death of a child, parent, or sibling. Fear may have captured their conscience. Maybe they sadly embraced lies about themselves and others. Compassion does not justify bad behavior, but looks for reasons why.

> **A Point to Ponder:** *Forgiveness is easier when we see others through eyes of compassion.*

Forgiveness Releases Another from Restitution

One childhood adventure I enjoyed was visiting my great uncle's country home that overlooked a large pond teeming with hungry fish. I learned how to bait a hook, wet a hook, and very carefully remove a bream or bass off a hook. Today, I relax and smile as I reflect on those lazy summer days. For me, the most wonderful time was an hour before sunset. As I sat under the canopy of a brilliant blue sky, seeing cattails at the far end of my outdoor sanctuary, I was serenaded by a chorus of bullfrogs, the warm-up band for the Lord's main performance of a star-studded sky.

When I could no longer see my cork bobbing in the water, I retreated back to the house. My great uncle was a bachelor. The main floor of his modest ranch home smelled dingy with a hint of plastic, which covered his living room furniture. Years later my grandmother invited her brother to live at her place. In that home, there was a narrow door in the kitchen that led down to a scary cellar. My uncle moved into that space: a dim, damp, cold, dungeon-like man cave. It was a mess—empty beer cans, cluttered clothes, and nauseating body odor. Upstairs was light, love, and the aroma of cathead biscuits, white gravy, and fried chicken. A contrast between life and death.

The depressing, dark cellar reminds me of how I mentally and emotionally place people in the unmerciful part of my heart. I lock them up to punish them or forget about them. Thankfully, the Holy Spirit relentlessly convicts me to truly forgive, which means I unlock the door that leads to the dark place of my soul, go down the steps, unshackle my offender, look at them with compassion, and lead them back up the stairs into the light of the main floor of my life. With a genuine, gentle tone, I say, "I forgive you for [the offense] and I want us to have a healthy, growing relationship." God's grace clears away dense hurt from deep within my thoughts and emotions, allowing me to embrace friends with mercy and love.

Who is locked up in the cellar of your soul that you can release, meet with, and forgive? Wisdom in leadership does not allow hurt from the past to drive demanding, detrimental behavior in the present. Forgiveness sets us and our offenders free to love and serve others in Jesus's name.

TAKEAWAY: *Forgiving leaders lovingly meet their offenders and forgive specific sins.*

What About People You Have Offended?

"Therefore, if you are offering your gift at the altar and there remember that your brother or sister has something against you, leave your gift there in front of the altar. First go and be reconciled to them; then come and offer your gift" (Matthew 5:23-24).

Jesus described a worshipper who had come to offer a gift to God, but who had wounded a relationship with a brother or a sister. Their gift was unacceptable to the Lord until the one presenting the gift was reconciled to the offended person—who is more valuable to God than the offering. It is inconsistent to seek reconciliation with God without first seeking reconciliation with those the Lord has placed in our lives. We ask forgiveness from the one we offended on earth before we ask forgiveness from God in heaven.

When you're trying to pray or worship, what disconnected

relationship comes into your mind? Who has the Holy Spirit laid on your heart; who has something against you? Maybe you made an insensitive remark that hurt a friend. Or you forgot to invite someone to a special occasion, and they felt ignored and rejected. Perhaps a business relationship went awry and you need to ask forgiveness and offer restitution. Go quickly, humble yourself, and ask forgiveness. The amount of time it takes to seek reconciliation is an indicator of how close your walk with Christ is.

"We love because he first loved us. Whoever claims to love God yet hates a brother or sister is a liar. For whoever does not love their brother and sister, whom they have seen, cannot love God, whom they have not seen. And he has given us this command: Anyone who loves God must also love their brother and sister" (1 John 4:19-21).

A Point to Ponder: Our worship is most authentic when our relationships have been made whole.

Forgiveness cannot sit still until hearts are healed. Initiative accompanies love. Sometimes it is helpful to write out what you are feeling and how you want to express your contrite heart. You may or may not send the written note, but at the very least it can be a guide for your conversation. Moreover, make sure to own your offense by not saying, "*If* I have offended you." Instead say, "Please forgive me for hurting you. I was mad. My tone was wrong. I apologize." Godly sorrow goes a long way toward facilitating forgiveness from the one offended.

Yes, your efforts to reconcile may be rebuffed, but you can only give up on someone when your Savior Jesus has given up on them. Also, your restitution may be required before reconciliation will take place. Pray about ways for you to replace what your friend lost. Like Zacchaeus (see Luke 19:8), be extremely generous in how you make things right. Most of all, you honor Christ when you take the time to be His minister of reconciliation.

"Therefore, if anyone is in Christ, the new creation has come: The old has gone, the new is here! All this is from God, who reconciled us to himself through Christ and gave us the ministry of reconciliation: that God was reconciling the world to himself in Christ, not counting people's sins against them. And he has committed to us the message of reconciliation" (2 Corinthians 5:17-19).

Heavenly Father, give me the courage and conviction to seek out those I offend and ask for their forgiveness.

TAKEAWAY: *Forgiving leaders go to those they have offended, apologize, and ask for forgiveness.*

Have You Really Forgiven Yourself?

"Therefore, there is now no condemnation for those who are in Christ Jesus" (Romans 8:1).

Have you forgiven yourself? Have you really forgiven yourself? We know we have forgiven ourselves if we are free from guilt and self-condemnation. Otherwise we are stuck in a crazy cycle of reliving bad decisions that are in the past and cannot be changed. Living in continual guilt will never clear our consciences about past mistakes. Only when we forgive ourselves will we be set free from guilt and shame.

When we do not release ourselves from the guilt of previous indiscretions, we try to make up for it by overcompensating in the present. Perhaps you neglected your children in their early years, so now when they are older you've tried to make up for it by letting them do what they please, thus enabling poor decisions. Instead, they need to experience the consequences of bad behavior so they can learn and grow into responsible adults and citizens.

Jesus told the story of a loving father who allowed his son to hit bottom. As a consequence the son came to understand and take responsibility for his reality: "When he came to his senses, he said, 'How many of my father's hired servants have food to spare, and here I am starving to death! I will set out and go back to my father and say to him: Father, I have sinned against heaven and against you'" (Luke 15:17-18).

A Point to Ponder: *Forgive yourself in the same manner your Master Jesus has forgiven you.*

Forgiving yourself begins by embracing the truth that your heavenly Father has forgiven you. The grace of God is in abundant supply; no one is beyond its reach. The Lord loves you unconditionally, and He forgives the objects of His love. Has the grace of God seeped deep into your soul, so you know you are set free from the guilt and shame of sin? If not, accept His forgiveness and then forgive yourself, and trust the Lord to make up for what has been lost.

"In him we have redemption through his blood, the forgiveness of sins, in accordance with the riches of God's grace" (Ephesians 1:7).

When you forgive yourself, you are able to forgive others. Self-forgiveness is a key to unlocking real relationships. Authentic community with Christ and Christians comes from forgiveness from your heavenly Father, forgiveness from others, and forgiveness from yourself. What have you not released yourself from? Lay it on the altar of God's grace, and He will remove it by His eternal fire of forgiveness and love.

"This is the first and greatest commandment. And the second is like it: 'Love your neighbor as yourself'" (Matthew 22:38-39). When you love yourself—you forgive yourself!

How can I grow in my love and forgiveness of myself? How does God forgive me?

TAKEAWAY: *Forgiving leaders forgive themselves so they can be free from guilt and shame.*

Forgiveness is a big deal. It is a big deal to God and should be a big deal to those of us who follow Christ. Prayerfully, the Lord will use our forgiveness to point others to His forgiveness.

Summary of Chapter Nine Takeaways

1. Forgiving leaders engage in the process of confession, repentance, and forgiveness.

2. Forgiving leaders embrace humility as a precondition for forgiveness.

3. Forgiving leaders have abundant forgiveness even for those who hurt them the most.

4. Forgiving leaders are chronically grateful for ongoing forgiveness from God.

5. Forgiving leaders forgive others to the extent they have been forgiven by Christ.

6. Forgiving leaders freely forgive others, and enjoy forgiveness from their Lord Jesus.

7. Forgiving leaders lovingly meet their offenders and forgive specific sins.

8. Forgiving leaders go to those they have offended, apologize, and ask for forgiveness.

9. Forgiving leaders forgive themselves so they can be free from guilt and shame.

Chapter Ten

Learning to Lead Like Jesus with Encouragement

*Encourage one another and build each
other up, just as in fact you are doing.*

1 Thessalonians 5:11

*We need each other for the moments when we've
got to borrow the strength of each others' words,
borrow a friend's faith that lifts us up, borrow a little
encouragement just to carry us through the day.*

Ann Voskamp

Jesus Was Encouraging

When a Samaritan woman came to draw water, Jesus said to her, 'Will you give me a drink?' (His disciples had gone into the town to buy food.) The Samaritan woman said to him, 'You are a Jew and I am a Samaritan woman. How can you ask me for a drink?' (For Jews do not associate with Samaritans.) Jesus answered her, 'If you knew the gift of God and who it is that asks you for a drink, you would have asked him and he would have given you living water'" (John 4:7-10).

Jesus went out of His way to bring much-needed encouragement to a woman (the culture gave women a second-class status) who was a Samaritan (a race looked down on by Jews). He honored her by asking for refreshment. She was startled that He would break the taboo and speak to her, but her attention was held captive as He offered her living water. Jesus was always on the lookout to give others encouragement, especially those who suffered under the burden of bias and injustice. Encouragement goes out of the way to help others find the right way.

What Is Encouragement?

Encourage is from the Greek word *parakaleo*, which means to implore, so encouragement is not shallow sentiment or praise, but instead helping others become better. It's mentioned 115 times in the Bible. While it is a spiritual gift, all of us can be encouragers. We can instill courage in someone who may need just a little, to get them through life's challenges.

Everyday Encourager: Truett Cathy

"Therefore encourage one another and build each other up, just as in fact you are doing" (1 Thessalonians 5:11).

One of the best encouragers I have ever known was Truett Cathy, the founder of Chick-fil-A restaurants. He was a father figure to hundreds of foster children, a generous giver, a faithful husband, an engaged dad, a loyal friend, and a loving leader. Truett famously said on many occasions, "How do you know if someone needs encouraging? If they are breathing." Every living person is a candidate for an infusion of courage!

I was honored and blessed to be one of several thousand who attended Truett's funeral in 2014. I arrived two hours early and sat 40 feet from the casket. I was there out of deep respect and to support my friend Woody Faulk, who was one of the speakers. Hundreds of others watched via video in the overflow area and in the Chick-fil-A staff offices. News reporters gathered outside, but what took place inside was a piece of history that only a Jesus follower could fully appreciate. Truett represented goodness, common sense, and decency. He was not a celebrity, but a servant. Though we only met twice, I wept, because I felt I had lost a friend whom I loved deeply.

After the two-hour celebration of Truett's homegoing, I whispered this prayer from my heart: "Heavenly Father, like Your humble servant, I want to finish well for Your glory. Use me every day to give someone courage—*the gift of encouragement*—to face whatever challenges they face. In Jesus's name, Amen!"

TAKEAWAY: *Encouraging leaders look every day for ways to encourage those they meet.*

No One Has Ever Complained of Too Much Encouragement

Have you ever felt taken for granted? Undervalued or underappreciated? Troublemakers and loud people who live for the limelight seem to get all the attention, and maybe you are left unnoticed since you offer no drama. But when we stop to reflect on our relationships, we realize we all want to know if we meet the expectations of others. Marriage, work, family, and friendships all require two-way communication to ensure everyone understands each other, appreciates each another, and sets each other up for success. Even the most faithful need to know they are known and loved by those who lead them. Courage is contagious.

We all suffer from a courage deficiency. Everyday life sucks courage from each one of us. So a daily dose of vitamin E—encouragement—is the healthiest supplement. It is hard to count the number of ways we are assaulted by discouragement. We're hit with horrific world headlines of terrorism, disease, and drought. Some face personal challenges related to health issues, rebellious children, financial stress, relational conflict, sexual abuse, emotional hurt, anger, or spiritual brokenness. Human beings were created by God with an innate daily need for courage from other human beings. An infusion of courage into a heart germinates hope and helps people persevere.

A Point to Ponder: A little bit of encouragement goes a long way to give hope for life's journey.

What Are Some Ways to Genuinely Encourage People?

Encouragement comes in a variety of forms: kind words, a warm smile, a thoughtful handwritten note, a timely text with a prayer and Scripture verse, a generous gift, an invitation to spend time together, listening—or an intimate, quiet meal seasoned with caring conversation. I cannot remember anyone ever complaining about receiving too much encouragement. On the other hand, I have seen some of the best workers wander away because they felt underappreciated and overworked! For those we live with, perhaps we can intentionally seek to understand what brings them alive, and then offer encouragement in those forms.

Some appreciate public praise—so praise them publicly. Others are helped by private correction—so correct them privately. Yet others most appreciate a financial reward—so reward them financially. One might want you to show up for what's important to them—so show up for that. Another might be most blessed if you would read a book that impacted their life—so read the life-changing book. Discover what encourages another and deliver that item!

Wisdom in leadership looks for ways to love those they serve, by taking the time to value, care for, and spend time with them. That allows both to see, hear, and experience encouragement. Courage is best infused through healthy relationships. Someone with a hungry or heavy heart can gain the confidence to move ahead because their leader is right with them to provide strength and courage. Perseverance, kindness, joy, gratitude, hope, and faith are all fruits of encouragement.

> **TAKEAWAY:** *Encouraging leaders are prayerful givers of customized courage.*

My Need for Courage When Facing Prostate Cancer

When I was first confronted with the news of my early-stage prostate cancer, I was extremely discouraged! I was mad, sad, and afraid. I was mad at the Lord because I didn't think I had time for a major health distraction. I was too busy doing His work. How could He slow me down and put me on the sideline? I was sad because I wanted to see our grandbabies grow up and come to know Jesus. I wanted to go to their soccer games, take them on trips, attend their high school and college graduations, and sit on the front row at their weddings.

I was afraid of dying—the pain, the process, and the people left behind who need me. I had lost courage. I was overwhelmed by the cancer treatment choices. Robotic? Scalpel? Radiation? Proton? HIFU (High Intensity Focused Ultrasound)? I was a desperate candidate for encouragement. Then the doctor reminded me, "You have three months to choose a treatment."

Ninety days to decide something that would determine the rest of my life? My fears filled in the blanks of the worst-case scenarios. I would become totally impotent. No more physical intimacy with my wife, at age 52! Total incontinence. I would be unable to control my urination—really? A bag tied to my hairy leg and filled with warm urine, emptied multiple times a day—you have to be kidding me. Aaaaargh!

Yes, fear and pride got the best of me. I've always been very, very active. I still possessed the energy of a younger man. A former high school football player, I enjoy tennis, hiking, walking, running, and all forms of exercise. My body still relished exertion and sweat. Now I was going to just shrivel up and become a big burden. No way, Lord!

I ended up being the only one who attended my pity party. It all came to a head as I was within minutes of going in for my biopsy to confirm or dismiss my cancer. Though the procedure would take only 20 minutes, it would be very uncomfortable. It felt like an hour, as the doctor extracted ten tissue samples from strategic locations within my prostate. I was nervous and fearful, dreading having a metal intruder make its way through an orifice of my body that was not designed for this physical invasion. Like a cup of cold water surrounded by dry ice, fear had frozen my faith.

> **A Point to Ponder:** *Our pain is the Lord's opportunity to show up and show off.*

Encouragement from the Most Unlikely Place: "Are You the Guy?"

Then one of the most surreal God moments of my life occurred. Ten minutes before I was led back for my biopsy hell, in came a nice, middle-aged lady in dark blue scrubs, with a surgical mask dangling around her neck (we later learned she was the head nurse). I kid you not, she walked up to Rita and me and said, "Are you the guy who writes the Wisdom Hunters Daily Devotionals?"

I said "Yes"—sheepishly, because I was not feeling very spiritual or worthy of taking credit for any kind of confidence in Christ. In a warm, honest, and grateful tone, with love, she said, "I just had the worst 12 months of my life, and a year ago a friend of mine from Houston, Texas, emailed me a copy of the Wisdom Hunters devotional. God used those writings to keep me in His Word, and that daily encouragement from Him was how I was able to get through the past year!"

My precious Savior Jesus comforted me through His kind servant. As I was escorted back to my biopsy I had a renewed perspective of hope, faith, and fearlessness. The Holy Spirit spoke to my heart, "This illness is not about you, but about Me and My glory. It's about the doctors, nurses, hospital attendants, maintenance workers, family, friends, and everyone you meet—who need to see Jesus in your life. My dear son Boyd, I want to do a work in you, so I can do a work through you, so I can do a work with you!"

A Point to Ponder: When our discomfort intersects with God's comfort, we can comfort others.

Encouragement in Worship, and Financial Encouragement from Generous Friends

Fast-forward a few months. I experienced a successful five-hour, one time, less invasive treatment, with no radiation, no surgery, no chemotherapy, and no significant side effects. My Atlanta urologist, Dr. Kassabian, administered HIFU (High Intensity Focused Ultrasound) in Montreal, Canada. This wonderful option for treating early-stage prostate cancer is now approved by the FDA in the United States.

To expand on my story from chapter 7, after my outpatient treatment I experienced the most sublime encouragement from the Lord and comfort from my wife through praise and worship. To combat the severe pain and discomfort, Rita administered pain medication—prayer and modern medicine are a great combination! In the warmth of each other's embrace, we worshipped Almighty God to the hymn "How He Loves Us."

As previously shared, a phrase about afflictions and God's glory impacted me in a new way as never before. In the midst of worshipping,

I sensed a deluge of our heavenly Father's love as if poured out from overflowing buckets of water. He whispered His reassuring refrain to my heart, "I am with you, My son; I love you, Boyd."

Then came Kevin and David, two friends who proved to be wonderful, Christlike courage-givers at a crucial time. I discovered my unconventional treatment option—HIFU—was not covered by my medical insurance. Rita and I thought we would need to pull $50,000 from our very modest retirement funds, so after the 10 percent penalty and payment of income taxes, we would net $30,000 to cover the cost.

Unsolicited, and unaware of the others' interest, our new friend David very generously gave $15,000 out of his own pocket. Then Kevin asked 15 friends to give $1,000 each (non-tax-deductible gifts), so the entire cost of my medical procedure was covered by extraordinary, caring, loving friends and brothers in Christ! Jesus is King, but in the right moment, with the right motivation, cash can sure encourage somebody.

TAKEAWAY: *Encouraging leaders are generous givers of their time and money.*

Barnabas: a Leader Who Lived Up to His Name

The name Barnabas means "Son of Encouragement." His encouragement expressed itself in financial generosity, in not giving up on a quitter, in endorsing the unseemly character of a new Christian, and in a fiery zeal to share the gospel with unbelievers. He was a Levite, a member of the Hebrew tribe of Levi, so he likely assisted the priests in the Jewish temple and faithfully gave his tithes to support the ministry.

1. Barnabas gave courage by caring for others through financial generosity.

"Joseph, who was also named Barnabas by the apostles (which is translated Son of Encouragement), a Levite of the country of Cyprus, having land, sold it, and brought the money and laid it at the apostles' feet" (Acts 4:36-37 NKJV).

When Barnabas saw the poor and needy doing without, he took his surplus—his land, a noncash asset—found a buyer, and converted his dirt to cash. Without hesitation he placed the funds at the feet of the faithful leaders he trusted, who under God's authority would apply the money where the needs were the greatest. Perhaps the real estate had been in his family for generations, or perhaps it was an investment he made in his lifetime. Either way, he experienced the joy of generosity while he was alive, instead of risking a misuse of assets after his death. He did his giving while he was living, so he was knowing where it was going. Barnabas gave financial courage to care for those in need. He offered his gift as an act of worship and gratitude to God.

2. Barnabas gave courage and extended loyalty to a struggling colaborer.

"Barnabas wanted to take John, also called Mark, with them, but Paul did not think it wise to take him, because he had deserted them in Pamphylia and had not continued with them in the work. They had such a sharp disagreement that they parted company. Barnabas took Mark and sailed for Cyprus" (Acts 15:37-39).

Mark and Barnabas were cousins (Colossians 4:10), so maybe that is one reason the Son of Encouragement was slow to give up on him. He was able to give his relative, also a brother in Christ, another chance. Mark's track record was not stellar. He had the reputation of being a quitter because of his past experience of leaving Paul and Barnabas mid-trip and heading back home.

But Barnabas didn't see Mark as a chronic quitter. Rather he saw someone whose past lapse of judgment could be corrected and mended by another opportunity to prove himself as one who could persevere in the face of difficulties. Barnabas took a chance by offering Mark a second chance. Grace does not tire in giving others courage to continue.

3. Barnabas gave courage and support to a leader with a suspicious history.

"When he [Saul] came to Jerusalem, he tried to join the disciples, but they were all afraid of him, not believing that he really was a disciple. But Barnabas took him and brought him to the apostles. He told them how Saul on his journey had seen the Lord and that the Lord had spoken to him, and how in Damascus he had preached fearlessly in the name of Jesus" (Acts 9:26-27).

Barnabas was not afraid to risk his character's capital in endorsing a new Christian with the reputation of persecuting, even killing Christians. In spite of the high risk in this relationship, he brought Saul before the apostles and testified of his genuine conversion to Jesus. A faithful leader is able to see the positive potential in a suspect leader who comes with a damaged reputation. Barnabas didn't discount Saul's need for discipleship and maturity, but he also didn't disqualify him because of his sinful, murderous behavior before conversion to Christ.

A faithful leader may prayerfully endorse another broken leader, trusting God to grow them in humility, grace, and holiness. A high-risk investment in a flawed but potentially faithful leader can result in eternal returns for the gospel of Jesus.

4. Barnabas gave courage without distorting the gospel.

"The rest of the Jews joined him [Peter] in this hypocrisy [ignoring their knowledge that Jewish and Gentile Christians were united, under the new covenant, into one faith], with the result that even Barnabas was carried away by their hypocrisy. But when I saw that they were not being straightforward about the truth of the gospel, I told Cephas (Peter) in front of everyone, 'If you, being a Jew, live [as you have been living] like a Gentile and not like a Jew, how is it that you are [now virtually] forcing the Gentiles to live like Jews [if they want to eat with you]?'" (Galatians 2:13-14 AMP).

An encourager might be tempted to allow the need for acceptance—relational harmony—to erode the need to clearly state the truth. Peter and Barnabas, in an attempt to appease their Jewish Christian friends, distorted the gospel by requiring non-Jewish believers (Gentiles) to embrace Jewish customs as part of their faith. Paul, with characteristic boldness, called out both of them for adding works to grace, implying the need for extra requirements for becoming a follower of Jesus. The missionary apostle was able to maintain an objective perspective about the pure gospel, and to clarify it in those early years of the church.

Emotionally charged and relationally risky: This was a case study in how the truth of the gospel can stand against cultural distortions. Peter and Barnabas—genuine, faithful leaders—learned a valuable lesson, to not add to or take away from belief in the death, burial, and resurrection of Jesus (1 Corinthians 15:1-8) as the only qualification for becoming a Christian.

The best encouragement dispenses courage without distorting the truth of God's Word. Perhaps the bold encouragement you need to give is to clarify truth for a well-meaning but confused soul.

"I have spoken to you with great frankness; I take great pride in you. I am greatly encouraged; in all our troubles my joy knows no bounds" (2 Corinthians 7:4).

> **TAKEAWAY:** *Encouraging leaders take risks on flawed but potentially faithful leaders.*

5. Barnabas gave others the courage to remain true to the Lord.

"When he [Barnabas] arrived and saw what the grace of God had done, he was glad and encouraged them all to remain true to the Lord with all their hearts" (Acts 11:23).

Remain true to the Lord, for He has remained true to you. Remain true while others encourage you. Remain true because the grace of God compels you to. Remain true, for He knows what is best for you. Remain true because you know it is the right thing to do. Remain true because your obedience encourages others. Remain true, with all your heart, so the kingdom of God advances aggressively for His glory.

It is easy to sign up as a Jesus follower, but follow-through requires faithfulness, so remain true to your commitment to Christ. It does matter that you follow through for Him. It matters to Him, to you, to your family, and to your credibility. It matters to those you have encouraged, those you are encouraging, and those you will encourage. It matters that you remain true.

Satan will try to suppress your commitment by his limited power of disease, discouragement, and discontent. He wants you to forget God's faithfulness and fall into his trap of temptation. He wants you to walk away from your family and follow your own selfish desires. He wants you to think you are an exception to the rule of law and accountability. He will feed your pride until you starve humility into nonexistence.

Jesus said, "I know where you live—where Satan has his throne. Yet you remain true to my name. You did not renounce your faith in me" (Revelation 2:13).

The hand of the Lord is on those who remain true with all their hearts. However, He moves on from those who drift into hypocritical behaviors, pretending one thing and doing another. Begin by exposing any unauthentic living, and seek to reconnect with Christ and others.

> **A Point to Ponder:** *Remain true to God and others, especially when you don't know what to do.*

Encouragement in God's Grace with Prayer

The grace of God creates an environment of encouragement. You can encourage others to remain true because God's grace has been extended to you. Grace encourages faithfulness. Grace realizes there is room for mistakes but still offers opportunities to remain true. Failure and faith can coexist. Encouragers engage others on a heartfelt level. You have the opportunity to come alongside husbands and wives, friends and relatives, new and mature Christians.

You can encourage them to remain true to the Lord and to each other. Encouragement extends hope, rooted in a relationship with Jesus Christ. Your eternally based encouragement is not sentimental or shallow. It is a heavenly hope evidenced by answered prayer. You encourage others exponentially when you petition Christ on their behalf.

Cry out to your heavenly Father and ask that He keep your teenagers true to Him. Pray for your friend's body to be healed by the hand of God. Pray for married couples to learn how to love and respect each other under the influence of the Holy Spirit. Pray for single adults to remain true to God's heart. Pray for your pastor to remain true to his calling to follow hard after the Lord.

Ask God for opportunities to pray with those you are encouraging. Prayer's power for encouragement cannot be exhausted. Above all, receive encouragement from the Lord and others to remain true. Then simultaneously and spontaneously extend encouragement to others to also remain true with all their hearts. Remain true because there is no limit to what the Lord can do. Giving up is not for you.

> *Heavenly Father, by Your grace I remain true to You*
> *because You are truth.*

Who needs me to help them remain faithful to their faith in Jesus?

TAKEAWAY: *Encouraging leaders remain true to the Lord and encourage others to do the same.*

Little things may offer big encouragement, so don't dismiss small acts of kindness. A prayer, a listening ear, a coffee, a lunch, a financial gift, a recommendation, or time together are ways most of us can offer encouragement. Pray today about how you can become a Barnabas to a forgotten friend.

Summary of Chapter Ten Takeaways

1. Encouraging leaders look every day for ways to encourage those they meet.
2. Encouraging leaders are prayerful givers of customized courage.
3. Encouraging leaders are generous givers of their time and money.
4. Encouraging leaders take risks on flawed but potentially faithful leaders.
5. Encouraging leaders remain true to the Lord and encourage others to do the same.

Chapter Eleven

Learning to Lead Like Jesus
with Faithfulness

My servant Moses; he is faithful in all my house.

Numbers 12:7

Faithful servants never retire.
You can retire from your career,
but you will never retire from serving God.

Rick Warren

Jesus Was Faithful

L et us run with perseverance the race marked out for us, fixing our eyes on Jesus, the pioneer and perfecter of faith. For the joy set before him he endured the cross, scorning its shame, and sat down at the right hand of the throne of God. Consider him who endured such opposition from sinners, so that you will not grow weary and lose heart" (Hebrews 12:1-3).

Jesus ran His race through life well, and He finished well—He was faithful. When He was tempted as we are all tempted, He endured— He was faithful. Joyfully, as He faced opposition from sinners, He endured—He was faithful. When He faced death on the cross, He accepted it—He was faithful to the end. Jesus remained faithful, and now He is seated at the right hand of God. Because of Him, we are inspired and equipped to endure to the end, and to not grow weary and lose heart. Jesus has marked out our race for us, that we should persevere by fixing our eyes on Him, the Faithful One.

Remaining Faithful in the Good Times and in the Bad Times

My wife, Rita, shared with me this insightful fable:

A white stallion had rode into the paddocks of an old man and all the villagers congratulated him on such good fortune.

The old man had only offered this: "Is it a curse or a blessing? All we can see is a sliver. Who can see what will come next?"

When the white horse ran off, the townsfolk were convinced the stallion had been a curse. The old man lived surrendered and satisfied in the will of God alone: "I cannot see as He sees."

When the horse returned with a dozen more horses, the townsfolk declared it a blessing; yet the old man said only, "It is as He wills and I give thanks for His will."

Then the man's only son broke his leg when thrown from the white stallion. The town folk all bemoaned the bad fortune of that white stallion. And the old man had only offered, "We'll see. We'll see. It is as He wills and I give thanks for His will."

When a draft for a war took all the young men off to battle but the son with the broken leg, the villagers all proclaimed the good fortune of that white horse. And the old man said but this, "We see only a sliver of the sum. We cannot see how the bad might be good. God is sovereign and He is good and He sees and works all things together for good."[14]

Indeed, God is sovereign.

Faithfulness Flows from Faith

Faithfulness flows from a heart of faith. The more I get my eyes off my own limitations and get my eyes on the Lord and His unlimited capabilities, the more my faithfulness is forged. When I look to the Lord, my faithfulness grows from faith, not dreadful duty. Yes, there are days when I don't feel very spiritual—even defeated—but by faith I still seek to do the right thing, and hope for my emotions to catch up with my obedience. I am very grateful to Jesus that He is faithful when I am unfaithful; He is loyal when I am disloyal; and He is loving when I am unloving.

By God's grace we pray not for a dry, dutiful faithfulness, but for a faithfulness fueled by eager faith, dependent on the Lord.

A faithful leader is already successful. God calls leaders to be humble, faithful servants, in contrast to proud leaders who are only motivated by what they want. Faithfulness is so counter to what our culture clamors for in leaders: tall, dark, handsome, or thin, pretty, smart. But faithful—what does that even mean?

Faithful means to show up at work when I would rather be at home; to show up at a child's school event when I would rather be at work; to show up and care for my mother-in-law, who is a stroke victim, when it is inconvenient; or to show up for a volunteer responsibility when I don't feel like it. Faithful means staying committed to a relationship when I have been hurt or misunderstood. Faithfulness is day in and day out doing what's right, with a right attitude, motivated by right reasons.

A Point to Ponder: Faithfulness can celebrate the accomplishment of already being successful.

Moses modeled faithfulness as a leader in the face of not feeling at all sure of his ability to speak or to influence the people. Yet the Lord branded him as the most humble man on earth (Numbers 12:3), and it was out of his position of utter dependence on God that the Lord instilled courage in his heart to remain faithful.

Moses recognized his very real limitations as a communicator, so the Lord sent him a gifted spokesperson, his brother Aaron. God is resourceful! A faithful leader is not expected to be equipped with all the gifts, but to recognize their own limitations and surround themselves with other gifted leaders. Wisdom in leadership is faithful to its calling, giftedness, and abilities.

"For every house is built by someone, but God is the builder of everything. 'Moses was faithful as a servant in all God's house,' bearing witness to what would be spoken by God in the future. But Christ is faithful as the Son over God's house. And we are his house, if indeed we hold firmly to our confidence and the hope in which we glory" (Hebrews 3:4-6).

> **TAKEAWAY:** Faithful leaders walk by faith and trust the Lord with the things that are uncertain.

Faithful to Focus on Depth of Character

Character matters. It matters in big corporations, small businesses, Wall Street, Main Street, homes, churches, and government. Character creates moral authority that qualifies a leader to dispense their responsibilities with effectiveness. Coupled with wisdom, it is a life compass that provides direction and insight into wise decisions. Wisdom in leadership sees life experiences as opportunities to grow our character more like Christ's.

In the past, Lake Tahoe was one of our favorite spots in the entire world for my wife, Rita, and me to rest, reflect, and rejuvenate. Half of the lake is located in Nevada and the other half in California. Over the years we strategically enjoyed the six-dollar prime rib dinners on the Nevada side, while staying in a quaint and serene cabin on the California side.

During one of our first visits to Tahoe, I discovered some amazing facts about this stunningly beautiful body of water. It is positioned one mile high, with 72 miles of gorgeous shoreline and 39 trillion gallons of icy water, at an average depth of 990 feet. The glacial runoff contributes to 99.9 percent water purity. If you could pour the water in Lake Tahoe over the state of California, the entire land mass would be covered in 14.5 inches of water.

Suddenly—without warning—the Holy Spirit yanked on my heart with this thought: *The depth of our character determines the breadth of our influence.* The development of character and maturity happen over time. Our character grows as we understand and apply wisdom to everyday life experiences. There are no shortcuts to obtaining wisdom and discernment; they come in bite-size portions. When we are faithful to follow through on what seems trivial, and as we learn from our mistakes, we are wisdom candidates. Wisdom is not manufactured; rather, it marinates in the mind and heart until it seeps into our attitudes and actions.

Are you focused on the depth of your character? Or is it only on the surface—just saying the right things to get the most expedient results? Are you committed to the long-term discipline of overcoming adversity at work, home, and relationships so you truly push past immature thinking and develop a mature mind?

A friend once told me, "Boyd, you can move every two years for twenty years and have two years' experience ten times, or you can invest your life in one place and have twenty years' experience in one location."

Wisdom in leadership focuses on depth and trusts God for breadth.

Perhaps you could make an audit of your character:

> Is it growing, or is it stuck at the emotional level of a teenager?
>
> Is your standard of behavior mature, or does it still roam around like a partying college student?
>
> Have you embraced your responsibilities as a husband, wife, father, mother, son, daughter, friend, employee, or employer?

Your hard work, honesty, integrity, patience, generosity, and service are all evidence of a character that is not content with the status quo, but is moving forward in maturity.

Influence is a trait that some do not value, but the wise see as important. It's from a position of influence that the best leaders lead, the most effective statesmen govern, productive parents parent, winning coaches coach, and engaging teachers teach.

Now how about an audit of your influence:

> Who is in your circle of influence?
>
> How are you being intentional to influence them toward wise living?

Do you have the moral authority to lovingly challenge their unwise decisions?

Do you model for them how to grow in their character development?

Heavenly Father, by Your grace I will focus on the depth of our relationship, and I will trust You with the breadth of my influence.

TAKEAWAY: *Faithful leaders focus on depth of character and trust God for breadth of influence.*

Faithful to Stay Engaged in the Lord's Work After Retirement

In chapter 9, I discussed my fractured but healed relationship with my dad, George Bailey. In this final chapter I'm compelled to describe my friendship with George Morgan, my wise mentor. Around age 30, I first met this gentle soul. George worked for our church for a whopping salary of one dollar a year. Naturally this intrigued me, and since I was just starting out in my career, it was hard to relate to this radical approach to work without pay. As the church administrator, George was the first to arrive for work in the morning (after the maintenance team), and the last to leave in the evening. His work ethic was stellar, and his mild manner and focus on excellence was motivating, but what attracted me the most was his wisdom.

How blessed we were as an organization to have George on the team, bringing his years of business experience to the table, as we were planning the relocation of a 150-year-old downtown church. Needless to say, there were heated discussions and conflicting opinions. When you throw in the spiritual dynamics, we had a recipe for relational disaster and church disunity.

However, George, with wisdom and grace, continually navigated the discussions back to what was best for the whole, and what was best for serving the next generation. Because of his steady hand as a trusted manager and leader, we were able to make the transition over the next few years to a new campus, with relatively few relational casualties.

TAKEAWAY: *Faithful leaders remain in service for the Lord beyond their career retirement.*

Wise Leaders Are Faithful Financially

One day I found myself ignorant and confused about our family financial options for savings. Ten percent of my salary was deducted each pay period and invested quarterly with a financial firm. My head was swimming over what seemed like a plethora of options: stocks, bonds, mutual funds, annuities, and more. So, I set up an appointment to meet with George and get his investment advice. I wanted to hear financial planning wisdom from someone who could work full-time for one dollar a year. He must have made some prudent decisions that I could apply to my own family finances!

We soon met and, in wise fashion, George first asked about our net worth, which we calculated in minutes on the back of a napkin! Then he asked about our financial goals. Based on these factors, along with our age and an informal assessment of our financial risk tolerance, George suggested diversification around mutual funds and bonds. His suggestions were not dramatic and his strategies were not sexy, but his advice was sound. I have to tell you, over the years, when we've stuck to his financial counsel, we've prospered. Any time we've deviated, we've lost money. Suffice it to say, Rita and I now follow George's financial advice, together with the wisdom and accountability of trusted friends and wise financial advisors: Carol, David, Jess, and Kevin.

TAKEAWAY: *Faithful leaders have plans to manage money well, so money doesn't manage them.*

Faithful Leaders Gain Wisdom Over a Long Period of Time

Have you ever wondered about the secret formula to someone's success? Did it come from:

Where they went to school?
Who they had as mentors?
What they have read?

Where they have traveled?

What they have as their life plan?

As I watched George exhibit humility with boldness, leadership with love, service with sensitivity, and communication with care, I so wanted to ask him the secret to his incredible success as a wise leader. He graciously allowed me to meet again with him during work hours. I could hardly sleep the night before, anticipating I would soon learn the tips and techniques that would allow me also to work for one dollar a year someday!

The next day I made my way to George's corner office. My white, starched, button-down shirt; freshly dry-cleaned suit; and spit-shined, polished shoes were meant to communicate my focus and discipline, as I sought to learn from someone I respected and admired. Once we exchanged niceties, George asked me what I had on my mind.

I disclosed my admiration of his financial and professional success. I explained my desire to learn and apply wisdom like I saw personified in him. Mustering up the courage, I asked George directly where he obtained wisdom over the years for work, family, and relating to people. With pen and pad in hand, I waited for wise nuggets so I could begin applying them to my own life and career.

To my surprise George simply said, "Boyd, all I can say is for ten years I have read a chapter in Proverbs each day, based on the day of the month. It works well as there are 31 chapters that nicely follow the 30-31 days for most months. The insights I learned from my daily meditations gave me the knowledge, understanding, and wisdom to face life's issues and difficulties."

I was stunned at the simplicity of his strategy, and frankly this is all I remember from our conversation some 27 years ago. The genius behind George's challenge is the need for knowledge to intersect with experience, before it develops into genuine and lasting wisdom. We learn best when we feel the need to learn; our education comes in real-life situations. The more our minds are saturated in truth, the higher the probability that we'll be able to call on that truth when we face trouble, when we struggle with making a decision, or when we have relational challenges.

I took George's example of seeking wisdom daily over ten years as a personal challenge. So, from age 30 to 40, each day, with few exceptions, I read a chapter in Proverbs. I can't begin to explain to you how necessary those readings became in my everyday life. The timeless wisdom of Solomon spoke to life issues like love, forgiveness, sin, wisdom, foolishness, drinking, sex, marriage, parenting, work, planning, adultery, relationships, savings, debt, spending, prosperity, poverty, diligence, fear of God, pride, and humility—to name but a few.

In a sentence, here is what I learned from George and from my own pursuit of wisdom:

The fruit of wisdom follows the pursuit of wisdom.

This flies in the face of a culture that wants instant gratification. Wisdom is built over time, not created in a mental microwave. Regardless of your stage of life, come up with a process, a life rhythm, that builds knowledge, understanding, and wisdom. There is a famous story you have probably heard, where Jesus described two contrasting homebuilders: one who built on sand, and one who built on solid rock. And when the storms came, only the one with a strong foundation survived (see Matthew 7:24-27).

Wisdom is that strong life foundation that takes time and effort to establish, but its long-term ability to weather life's storms makes it a very worthwhile investment.

TAKEAWAY: *Faithful leaders pursue God and receive His wisdom on how to live life.*

Faithful Leaders Put into Practice What They Learn

"Therefore everyone who hears these words of mine and puts them into practice is like a wise man who built his house on the rock" (Matthew 7:24).

We learn truth so we can apply it to life. Unused truth expires and becomes stale. When you hear truth and put it into practice, you are being wise. When you hear truth and ignore its application, you are being foolish. Foolish is the person who acknowledges truth outwardly but never applies it inwardly. Their foundation for faithfulness is fragile, so when the winds of adversity swirl and blow, their character collapses under the crushing power.

Someone may show up for a Bible study or attend a soul-stirring retreat and hear truth but never change for the better. How can this happen? It happens when people do not follow through with what they learn is right and true. There is a disconnect between their heads and their hearts. The idea to stop bad habits and start new ones is rationalized away with convincing excuses. We deceive ourselves by saying, "I don't have enough time," "I'm not spiritual enough," "I'll get around to this one day," or "God will understand if I wait."

John described self-deception's effect: "We deceive ourselves and the truth is not in us" (1 John 1:8).

Truth and deception can never coexist. So, jettison deception and apply truth now. If you wait, you will wander from the application. Right now is the wisest time to receive His gift of grace and to graft it into your life. You are responsible for the truth you have received. Therefore, steward it wisely. Use it before you lose it. Become a practitioner of truth.

> **A Point to Ponder:** *A faithful life lives out what is applied to the heart and renewed in the mind.*

Wisdom in leadership applies truth in doses that can be integrated into your character. Do not be overwhelmed by the many things in your life that need to change. Choose one thing, such as loving your spouse with abandon and sensitivity. Paul said in Ephesians 5:25 that the husband should "[give] himself up" for his wife. Without saying a word, serve in secret so your spouse can experience your unselfish care and concern. Get into their world by loving them at their point of interest. It may relate to entertainment, cooking, or yard work. Whatever it may be, serve them in ways that tell them you care.

At work, you have the opportunity to put the radical teaching of Jesus into practice by treating others as you want to be treated (Matthew 7:12). Think of a colleague who let the team down and is in need of forgiveness. If you were in their shoes, you would appreciate a gift of mercy. You can put into practice the Golden Rule because you are golden, now that God has graced your life.

God has filled you with His grace so you can live a gracious life. Focus on building the foundation of your life and character, one brick of truth at a time. This architecture designed by the Almighty will endure. Leave a lasting legacy to your children by putting into practice what you know to be true. The teachings of Jesus are truth. Believe and apply. Put His principles into practice, and persevere.

TAKEAWAY: *Faithful leaders put into practice what they learn.*

Faithful Leaders Have Hearts Guarded by God's Peace

"Above all else, guard your heart, for everything you do flows from it" (Proverbs 4:23).

"How is your heart?" This is the question he asked me almost every time we talked, which was often. But I will not hear these words from him anymore in this life. Recently, after a two-and-one-half-year battle with cancer, Scott—my friend and fellow Wisdom Hunters board member—went to be with Jesus. I miss him. Selfishly, I long to hear his loving question: "Boyd, how is your heart?"

To me, Scott was a spiritual doctor who cared about my heart's condition. He knew the quality of my life depended on the health of my heart. He reminded me of my need for the Great Physician.

Scripture says everything flows from your heart—your hopes, your dreams, your fears, your anxieties, your anger, your forgiveness, your humility, your peace, your greed, your generosity, and your love. Yes, everything that makes you who you are comes from your heart. So, above all else, your heart needs a guard, and the best guard is God's peace.

When the Holy Spirit fills your heart by faith, He flushes out sin and leaves enough room for the fruit of the Spirit. Only a heart guarded by God's peace can withstand the influence of ungodliness. A heart submitted to Christ in prayer is protected by Christ with peace.

"The peace of God, which transcends all understanding, will guard your hearts and your minds in Christ Jesus" (Philippians 4:7).

A Point to Ponder: A heart guarded by God is guaranteed His peace.

Unhealthy heart conditions include:

- Faintheartedness

- Loss of heart

- A broken heart

- A foolish heart

- A hard heart

The remedy for these spiritual ailments is a whole heart for Jesus. You may feel fainthearted today—weary in your faith and work. If so, take time to slow down, rest, and allow the Holy Spirit to restore your heart to wholeness. A loss of heart is a reflection of hope deferred, which creates a sick soul condition. But hope in Christ gives your heart peace and reassurance.

Perhaps your heart is broken by past hurt or present rejection. Seek your heavenly Father to be forgiven and to forgive. Be on guard! A foolish heart forgets God or even stops believing God. Excessive worry can act like a form of atheism. When we are paralyzed by fear and anxiety, we are behaving as if God does not exist. So, we must guard against a foolish heart by gaining a heart of wisdom.

Most disturbing is a hard heart—someone jaded by injustice or the lack of integrity in others. Fortunately, by faith in Jesus, a hard heart can be replaced by a heart born from above. A heart from the Lord gives us a heart for the Lord.

So in honor of my friend Scott, let me ask you, friend: "How is your heart?"

"A good man brings good things out of the good stored up in his heart, and an evil man brings evil things out of the evil stored up in his heart. For the mouth speaks what the heart is full of" (Luke 6:45).

Heavenly Father, I ask that You would give me Your heart of love, grace, and forgiveness.

Which spiritual ailments do you have in your heart that need God's remedies?

TAKEAWAY: *Faithful leaders are vulnerable and share their hearts.*

Faithful Leaders Make Room for the Next Generation of Leaders

"The LORD said to Moses, 'Take Joshua son of Nun, a man in whom is the spirit of leadership, and lay your hand on him. Have him stand before Eleazar the priest and the entire assembly and commission him in their presence'" (Numbers 27:18-19).

After 16 years of leading Ministry Ventures, the Lord called me to serve on the National Christian Foundation team. God's will is always what's best for all parties, and I certainly experienced this in my career transition. Over a four-year period I saw more and more how it would be best for me to move on and make room for the success of the other Ministry Venture team leaders. If I remained in charge, the organization could not grow into a more sustainable, fee-based ministry soon enough. I was our greatest growth constraint. By God's grace I made the decision to move on and make more room for success.

Moses led Israel as far as he was able. God stated clearly that he was not the man to lead the people into the Promised Land. Instead, the Lord called Joshua, Moses's apprentice, to be his successor for Israel's next season of success. Joshua was a gifted leader who experienced the good, the bad, and the ugly under Moses's mentorship. Most of all, the younger leader observed the favor of God working through Moses. The leadership transition was respectful to all, and honored the Lord. Moses prayerfully laid hands on Joshua, commissioning him publicly.

"For this reason I remind you to fan into flame the gift of God, which is in you through the laying on of my hands" (2 Timothy 1:6).

> *A Point to Ponder: When we follow God's will, we are doing what's best for all involved.*

Do you need to make room for success by moving on? What's holding you back? The flesh loves to feel wanted, and in the process of self-absorption drives good people away. Our ego likes to enjoy the prominence of a position that others admire, but when our ambition becomes an idol, we miss the blessing of God's favor. It's better to transition under terms we can prayerfully influence and facilitate than to be forced out because we overstayed our welcome. Humility and faith make room for the success of others above our own agenda.

Do you need to step up into a more responsible leadership role so the organization can grow to the next level? What's holding you back? Fear of failure is like the common cold: There is no cure. If you feel a healthy sense of hesitation, take it as an opportunity to grow your faith in your team and in your intimacy with your heavenly Father. Leaders with no fear might not be realistic about what they face. Those the Lord calls, He equips with skills, He empowers with wisdom, and He encourages with results. Failure is an option for learners. So, step up and make room for success!

"David…enjoyed God's favor and asked that he might provide a dwelling place for the God of Jacob. But it was Solomon who built a house for him" (Acts 7:45-47).

Heavenly Father, I am willing to move on to make room for the success of others.

Where is the Lord calling me to step up with more responsibility for the success of the organization's mission?

TAKEAWAY: *Faithful leaders develop successors who can successfully lead to the next level.*

Faithful Leaders Finish Well

"So they hanged Haman on the gallows which he had prepared for Mordecai" (Esther 7:10 NASB).

Some people do not finish well and others do. Why? It comes down to our choices. The choices you make today determine how you will finish tomorrow. You can live in very difficult circumstances yet make very wise choices. If so, there is a great probability you will finish well. You can live in the best of conditions but make unwise choices. In that case, the chances are good that you will not finish well.

So, does it mean we will have no regrets when we finish well? No. God is not looking for perfection, but He does desire passion for Himself and obedience to His Word. People who do not finish well have decided to take control of things themselves. They act like they have a better plan than God. This type of decision-making will have limited, if any, success in the Lord's eyes.

Then how does the Bible describe finishing well? It's like a lifelong race—a marathon. Jesus is at the finish line, and as you run you are surrounded by an eternal entourage of people who have been faithful before you. Your Savior and His saints are praying for you and encouraging you to finish well. This is His will. Don't lose heart or become proud of heart. Keep your focus on the ultimate destination: the prize of Christ's commendation that awaits you.

"Therefore, since we are surrounded by such a great cloud of witnesses, let us throw off everything that hinders and the sin that so easily entangles. And let us run with perseverance the race marked out for us, fixing our eyes on Jesus, the pioneer and perfecter of faith. For the joy set before him he endured the cross, scorning its shame, and sat down at the right hand of the throne of God. Consider him who endured such opposition from sinners, so that you will not grow weary and lose heart" (Hebrews 12:1-3).

> *A Point to Ponder: We finish well when those who know us the best, love us the most.*

Along the race of life you will encounter difficulty. You will tire and need rest. There will be stretches of road where you run alone and feel like quitting. At other times the race will seem like an uphill battle, with every muscle in your body screaming for attention. But thankfully, there are times of refreshment and rejuvenation. After you have run up a hill of hope, there is an opportunity to enjoy the run down the other side. Indeed, some roads dead-end—you may need to regroup and study the map of God's will (Scripture).

Finishing well comes from living in the presence of God. Intimacy with Him positions you to hear His voice and obey Him. You want to please the one you love. And what about those who love you? Yes, caring for those who love you most facilitates finishing well. Listen intently to those who have your best interests in mind, who are finishing well themselves. We need mentors to help us focus on the right priorities.

Finishing well means you live like you are dying—because, in fact, we are all terminal cases. We should have a sense of urgency to live our lives today for Christ, since tomorrow may not come. We live best when we live as if today were our last day. Thus, finish well today for your heavenly Father, family, friends, and future saints.

A life well spent makes your Savior smile and say: "Well done, thou good and faithful servant" (Matthew 25:21 KJV).

What does it mean for me to finish well? Am I finishing well today?

TAKEAWAY: *Faithful leaders finish well.*

Are you on a path to finish well, or are you secretly flirting with a series of foolish decisions? Finish well today and you have a higher probability of finishing well tomorrow. Invite others to really know you and for you to know them.

Summary of Chapter Eleven Takeaways

1. Faithful leaders walk by faith and trust the Lord with the things that are uncertain.

2. Faithful leaders focus on depth of character and trust God for breadth of influence.

3. Faithful leaders remain in service for the Lord beyond their career retirement.

4. Faithful leaders have plans to manage money well, so money doesn't manage them.

5. Faithful leaders pursue God and receive His wisdom on how to live life.

6. Faithful leaders put into practice what they learn.

7. Faithful leaders are vulnerable and share their hearts.

8. Faithful leaders develop successors who can successfully lead to the next level.

9. Faithful leaders finish well.

Conclusion: Reflection, Prayer, and Application

Good questions can help you assess how you are learning to lead like Jesus. They can reveal why you need wisdom, what areas you need wisdom in, and ways to grow in wisdom. So here is a simple but serious exercise to help you better understand your wisdom gaps. Spend 30 minutes reflecting on and praying over the sets of questions below, and highlight the two or three questions you need to give attention to right now. Ask the Lord and He will lead you through this wisdom audit. I listed the 11 qualities modeled in the life of Jesus, with three sets of questions under each one. Take your time and discuss this with a few friends so you can learn from their insights also.

Ask the Holy Spirit to guide your heart, and ask God for wisdom. Imitate Christ's life and enjoy the journey of being a fellow wisdom hunter! (www.wisdomhunters.com)

Humility

1. Do you think about yourself more than other people when you are in their presence, or are you focused on their needs? What are some ways you can show someone you defer to them and prefer their desires above your own? How do humility and wisdom go together?

2. Do you expect to be served or to serve? Are you seeking to advance your kingdom or God's kingdom? How did Jesus live out humility in a way that is attractive and challenging? What does it mean to seek first God's kingdom? Why is it wise to seek God's kingdom first?

3. What evidence of humility is there in your life? What areas of your life would an honest friend say are prideful? How can you keep spiritual pride from causing you to look down on others? How does pride affect your ability to gain wisdom?

Love

1. Are you aware of how you are loved by your heavenly Father, so that it instills peace, comfort, and security into your heart? How does the Lord see you as His child? Is your identity based on God's love for you, or on other inferior, distorted, and undependable loves? How does Christ's love help you grow a heart of wisdom?

2. Do you love others conditionally or unconditionally? Is there someone who desperately needs your love, who is in a sorrowful season? Who do you need love from more than anyone else? How do you need for them to love you? How can wisdom help you to love in better ways?

3. Is it hard for you to love those who are different from you? How did Jesus relate to those different from Him? How does the Lord want you to love someone who does not understand you and perhaps you don't understand? Why is it wise to love your enemies?

Accountability

1. What does it mean to be truly accountable? Based on that definition, are you accountable? Who really knows you, and who do you really know? Why are you much wiser when you are accountable?

2. What risks do you take by not being authentically accountable? What area of your life needs accountability today? What is the wise thing to do about that? Who are three or four people you can invite to lovingly hold you accountable in specific areas of your life?

3. What does it mean to be accountable to the Lord? Is it enough just to be accountable to Him and no one else? Why do fear of the Lord and gaining wisdom go together? What will accountability to God look like at the judgment?

Relational

1. What is your plan to relationally invest in others? Why is this wise? What challenges do you face? How do you overcome these obstacles? What has been your greatest relational reward?

2. Who do you mentor, and who mentors you? Who is the wisest person you know at your work, whom you would like to spend more time with? Outside your work? In your family?

3. What are ways you can develop your relational skills? Who is gifted relationally that you can learn from? How did Jesus relate to His disciples? How did Christ model wisdom in His relationships? Why is it wise to grow your relational skills?

Teachable

1. What learning style motivates you and is effective for your growth and education? It might be an online class, attending lectures, interning with an expert, reading or listening to a book, or listening to a podcast. What types of wisdom would you like to study? Psalms, Proverbs, classic literature, or something else?

2. Who can you ask to join you in a book club to discuss big ideas and challenging thoughts? Why is it wise to hear other perspectives from a community of learners? How do their issues and solutions intersect with your life? Who is a wise elderly person you can learn from?

3. Jesus depended on His heavenly Father to tell Him what to do. Why was this wise? What process can you employ to learn from the Lord? What do you need wisdom for? Direction in your career? Insight into a relationship? Money management? Parenting?

Disciplined

1. Do your routines reflect a life in need of God's wisdom? Do you take time in the morning to reflect on truth and renew

your mind? Do you use your drive time or travel to listen to teaching, an inspiring life story, or uplifting worship? Do you have weekly calendar and budget planning to wisely manage your life? Why did Jesus talk more about money than any other topic?

2. Your body is a reflection of your wise care or foolish abuse. Do your eating and drinking patterns reflect a healthy and moderate lifestyle? Do you rest properly or run yourself ragged? Do you schedule at least 30 minutes every day to walk, run, cycle, use an elliptical machine, or do some other sustainable form of exercise?

3. Consider this pattern as a financial goal for each paycheck: to give 10 percent, save 10 percent, hold 30 percent for taxes, and live on 50 percent. Avoid debt if at all possible. How does acknowledging God's ownership of everything make you a wiser manager of what you have?

Grateful

1. Gratitude is an attitude that gives life and extends life. How is thankfulness expressed in your life? Do you give verbal thanks? A thankful note, email, text, or voicemail? Why is it wise to also genuinely acknowledge another person's gratitude toward you?

2. Gratitude for your salvation in Christ is foundational for an attractive life of joy and peace. Would your friends say you show that kind of thankfulness? Is their thankfulness on the rise after being with you? Why is it wise to be grateful to God?

3. How did Jesus express gratitude? How did His humility support an attitude of gratitude? Are the people you consider wise also grateful? Why? Ask the elderly why gratitude is key. How does thankfulness contribute to quality of life and longer life?

Generous

1. Everyone can be generous; a one-dollar bill or a hundred-dollar bill are each candidates for generosity. How are you

generous with little or much? How do you feel when you give to others? What does wise money management look like for you? Do you have a giving plan?

2. How has God been generous to you? Since the Lord has given you everything you have, are you willing to give everything you have? Why are people drawn to the Lord when they experience your generosity? What does God think of you when you are generous? Jesus was an extravagant giver; what was behind His generosity? How did He give generously?

3. Giving money is the simplest and in some ways the easiest form of generosity. Why is it sometimes harder to be generous with your time? Your relationships? What did Jesus mean when He talked about various forms of greed? Why is generosity the best remedy for greed?

Forgiving

1. Giving and receiving forgiveness leads to freedom. Are you free right now? Whose forgiveness do you need to receive, and whom do you need to forgive? Why is it harder to forgive some more than others? To whom do you need to extend a specific apology?

2. How has God forgiven you? Fully or partially? God's forgiveness of your sins for salvation is full, free, and irrevocable. Why does He not forgive your sins if you do not forgive others their sins against you? What happens to your heart when it's layered with unforgiven sins? Wouldn't you rather have a clean heart and a clear conscience?

3. Have you truly forgiven yourself from past sin and shame? Ask the Lord if you are holding on to anything unhealthy. If so, let it go. Inhale Christ's forgiveness and exhale His love, joy, and peace. When you experience God's great forgiveness, you forgive much and love much.

Encouraging

1. Are you a giver of courage or a taker of courage? Are people

glad to see you, hoping you will encourage them and challenge them to become better? Do you lead by influence or by intimidation? How did Jesus encourage the disciples when He washed their feet?

2. How do you like to be encouraged? Do you have a Barnabas (an encourager) in your life? What did Truett Cathy mean when he said, "You can tell someone needs encouragement—if they are breathing"? Is it possible to encourage someone too much? How?

3. What are some ways the Lord encourages you? What are you facing for which you need to take courage and trust in Christ? How can another person's prayers be the greatest encouragement? What is your process of encouraging people with your prayers for them?

Faithful

1. What does it mean for you to finish well? How do you want those who know you the best to remember you the most? What do you want as your epitaph? Why is it wise to be faithful? Whom do you admire that lived a faithful life? What motivated them? How can you learn from their example?

2. What is your life purpose? My life purpose is "To love God by being a faithful husband, engaged father, loyal friend, and loving leader." Write in a sentence or two your life purpose. Why do some leaders, even wise leaders like Solomon, not finish well? What happens?

3. How was Jesus faithful to the end? What motivated Him to finish well? What did Christ mean when in agony He prayed, "Not My will but Yours be done"? What themes in the life of Jesus facilitated His faithfulness? Consider how humility, love, accountability, relationships, teachability, discipline, gratitude, generosity, forgiveness, and encouragement all facilitated Christ's faithfulness. What quality in Jesus's life is He calling you to focus on in your life?

How to Become a Disciple of Jesus Christ

J esus came to them and said, 'All authority in heaven and on earth has been given to me. Therefore go and make disciples of all nations, baptizing them in the name of the Father and of the Son and of the Holy Spirit, and teaching them to obey everything I have commanded you. And surely I am with you always, to the very end of the age'" (Matthew 28:18-20).

Holy Scripture teaches us how to become disciples and how to make disciples.

Believe

Belief in Jesus Christ as your Savior and Lord gives you eternal life in heaven.

> If you declare with your mouth, "Jesus is Lord," and believe in your heart that God raised him from the dead, you will be saved (Romans 10:9).

Obey

Obedience is an indicator of our love for the Lord Jesus and His presence in our life.

> Jesus replied, "Anyone who loves me will obey my teaching. My Father will love them, and we will come to them and make our home with them" (John 14:23).

Repent and Be Baptized

To repent is to turn from your sin and then publicly confess Christ in baptism.

Repent and be baptized, every one of you, in the name of
Jesus Christ for the forgiveness of your sins. And you will
receive the gift of the Holy Spirit (Acts 2:38).

Worship, Prayer, Community, Evangelism, and Study

Worship and prayer express our gratitude and honor to God, and
our dependence on His grace. Community and evangelism show our
accountability to Christians and compassion for non-Christians. We
study to apply the knowledge, understanding, and wisdom of God.

Every day they continued to meet together in the temple
courts. They broke bread in their homes and ate together
with glad and sincere hearts, praising God and enjoying
the favor of all the people. And the Lord added to their
number daily those who were being saved (Acts 2:46-47).

Love God

Intimacy with Almighty God is a growing and loving relationship.
We are loved by Him, so we can love others and be empowered by the
Holy Spirit to obey His commands.

Jesus replied: "'Love the Lord your God with all your heart
and with all your soul and with all your mind.' This is the
first and greatest commandment" (Matthew 22:37-38).

Love People

Our love for others flows from our love for our heavenly Father. We
are able to love because He first loved us.

The second is like it: "Love your neighbor as yourself"
(Matthew 22:39).

Make Disciples

We disciple others because we are grateful to God and to those
who discipled us, and we want to obey Christ's last instructions before
going to heaven.

The things you have heard me say in the presence of many
witnesses entrust to reliable people who will also be qualified to teach others (2 Timothy 2:2).

Appendix A

Becoming a Leader of No Reputation

R. Scott Rodin

[*A brief note from Boyd Bailey:* I have one last gift for you, which comes from my friend Scott Rodin—his essay "Becoming a Leader of No Reputation" is by far my favorite article on leadership. I have shared his heartfelt writing with hundreds of leaders over the past 15 years and regularly reread for my own renewal and reminder of what it means to lead like Jesus. This article originally appeared in the *Journal of Religious Leadership*, Vol. 1, No. 2 (Fall 2002), pp. 105-119.

If you read only this essay, it will be worth having the book for future reference. Enjoy! Thank you again, Scott, for your permission to include your transformational words in *Learning to Lead Like Jesus*.]

I have been asked to reflect on my five years in the presidency at Eastern Baptist Theological Seminary, and to do so honestly, I need to begin with a confession. I was wrong. That is the most accurate statement I could make in summing up my experience in this position. Mind you, I was not wrong about everything. In fact, I believe we were quite right and accurate about a lot of things we attempted and accomplished during my tenure. I could make the usual list of "legacy" items that we former presidents do in justifying our term in office. There is much to be thankful for, many moments to treasure and certainly a legacy that I trust will make a difference to generations of students and faculty at our seminary.

Yet at the very heart of my reflection on my service lies this one major conclusion...I was wrong. I was wrong in my understanding and preconceived notions of leadership in Christian ministry. I was wrong in my expectations of others and myself. And I was wrong in my motivations, which may be the hardest thing to admit.

I look back and wonder why I was so wrong. My career path had certainly prepared me for leadership in an educational setting: twelve years of fundraising experience, a Ph.D. from a leading school in Great Britain, work in educational administration and a knack for strategic planning and vision casting. I had good experience in managing effective teams and working with not-for-profit boards. And my four years at the seminary as VP for Advancement had introduced me to the idiosyncrasies of theological higher education, which I felt I had negotiated quite well. There was no lack of preparation for the task.

Nor was there a lack of motivation. I had long believed that God had gifted me for leadership. I rose naturally and quickly into key leadership positions wherever I had gone. It felt right, seemed natural and was usually satisfying and challenging. So it was a logical move to take a top spot in theological education.

My problem was not with preparation, motivation, or even with a sense of true calling and a sincere desire to serve God with the best of my skills and abilities. The problem lay solely with my pre-determined understanding of what Christian leadership is really all about.

Five years ago, if you had asked me for a Scripture that epitomized the leadership ideal, I would likely have pointed you to Nathan's directive to King David, "Whatever you have in mind, go ahead and do it, for the Lord is with you" (2 Samuel 7:3). I could identify with David as "God's man at God's time" and I believed that God would pour out His wisdom and favor if I could be such a man. After all, there were kingdoms to conquer and people to be led. There were great things to be done for the Lord and no vision was too limited and no goal too small.

Now, five years later, I would point to a different verse. In speaking of Jesus' incarnation, Paul tells us "he made himself a man of no reputation, taking on the very nature of a servant" (Phil 2:7). The verse does not say that Jesus became a man of bad reputation, or questionable reputation, but simply of "no reputation. That is, reputation, image, prestige, prominence, power, and other trappings of leadership were not only devalued, they were purposefully dismissed. Jesus became such a man. Not by default or accident, but by intention and design. And it was only in this form that He could serve, love, give, teach, and yes, lead.

In reflecting on these past five years, I have come to believe that true Christian leadership is an ongoing, disciplined practice of becoming a person of no reputation, and thus, becoming more like Christ in this unique way. In his reflections on Christian leadership, Henri Nouwen refers to this as resisting the temptation to be relevant. He says, "I am deeply convinced that the Christian leader of the future is called to be completely irrelevant and to stand in this world with nothing to offer but his or her own vulnerable self."[15] Five years ago I rejected this idea outright. In doing so, I was wrong. Today I see and affirm this important notion that lies at the heart of godly leadership.

I will speak here to five areas where I have begun to learn what it is to be this sort of Christian leader. In each area I found that I began with a misunderstanding of what true Christian leadership looked like, and I have been on a journey of transformation, introducing me to a new way to serve as Christ taught us to serve.

Anointed vs. Appointed

I know of few Christian leaders today who were anointed before they were appointed. We have employed the business model of doing careful searches looking for Christian leaders whom we can appoint to office. We check their credentials, put them through rigorous interviews, and even give them psychological tests before we make the critical appointment. Once in place, we then anoint them and ask God to bless their work.

The Biblical evidence seems to indicate that God selects leaders in the opposite order. Samuel anointed David before appointing him King. The selection criterion for leadership was not based on who would most likely get the appointment, but whom God had anointed for this task. And appointment without anointment always led to disaster.

In 1997, I was satisfied that I had met the criteria for the job and was pleased to be appointed for the position of president. And while our board said a lovely prayer and laid hands on me, in retrospect I think the process was backward. No one asked me if I sensed God's anointing for this position. I don't know what I would have answered, but the issues and criteria to consider in forming an answer to this question were ones that I never considered in my response to my appointment.

The reason that anointing is so critical to the task of Christian leadership lies in its nature as the most unique form of leadership on earth. Christian leadership requires nothing less than a complete, wholesale sell-out of your life in service to God and God only. It is the "losing of your life" to the work God will do in you to benefit your institution, school, church or organization. And the stakes are high. Nowhere else in the Christian life will the price for divided loyalties be so costly for so many for so long. Ineffective and fallen leaders compromise kingdom work, and the effects are eternal. Therefore, it is a field that must be entered with the utmost seriousness, and only when one has clearly been anointed for the task.

With God's anointing comes God's power and presence. There is a special blessing bestowed on God's anointed. It is the blessing of God's power manifest in ways only seen through the work of God's chosen. God's anointed shout and walls fall. They lift their feeble staff and seas part. They speak God's word boldly and movements are begun that free men's souls. God's anointed do the miraculous because they are the servant of the Almighty. There is a unique presence of God in the lives of those God anoints and calls to leadership through that anointing. Without it, we are continually thrown back upon ourselves to make things work. With it, we have the resources of heaven at our disposal if we will be the faithful servant.

For this reason, God's anointed are incredibly unique people. God's anointed will do anything God asks...anything. God's anointed will seek God's will with a passion. They will not move without it and they will not be diverted from their course once they have it. God's anointed will love what God loves and hate what God hates. That means loving God's people, God's church, God's environment, God's resources, and God's plan. It also means hating sin in every form and coming against anything that stands between God's loving plan and its accomplishment. God's anointed are people of keen discernment, they are branches who are solidly engrafted into the true vine. God's anointed are servants first, last and always. And God's anointed have only one passion, to know and do God's will that He might have the glory. In this way, God's anointed are people of no reputation.

I did not come into my leadership position with a clear sense of anointing but in these past five years I have come to better understand and value the distinction between appointment and anointment.

Fighting the Need to Increase

When John the Baptist saw Jesus walking in his presence, he made the declaration, "He must increase, but I must decrease." Most Christian leaders would say that in their hearts they would wish that Jesus would increase and they would decrease. But it is hard to decrease in a leadership position. There are natural trappings that distinguish those in leadership such as salary, title, prestige, priority, power, influence, honor and advancement. And in each area there are tempting opportunities for increase. There are also pressures to increase and motivations to build a kingdom in which we house our growing collection of leadership trappings. This desire for the fame and fortune of leadership must be met not only by resistance, but, according to John Adams, we must have "a habitual contempt of them."[16] Nouwen is even more direct,

> The way of the Christian leader is not the way of upward mobility in which our world has invested so much, but the way of downward mobility ending on the cross...Here we touch the most important quality of Christian leadership in the future. It is not a leadership of power and control, but a leadership of powerlessness and humility in which the suffering servant of God, Jesus Christ, is made manifest.[17]

Perhaps the hardest place to decrease is in the influence and the power we hold over people and decisions. For this reason we find Christian leaders who are overly directive at best, and autocratic at worst. And as a result we produce churches and ministries that are rife with "learned helplessness." By overestimating our own worth, we help our people depend on us for everything. And that dependence feeds into our need to be needed, to be the "idea person" and visionary, and to be in control. We tell ourselves that the more we lead in this way, the more our leadership is valued and our presence desired.

Of course, this is not real leadership, but a counterfeit that gives us our increase and expands our kingdom. It also, however, does a terrible disservice to our people, leaving them uninvolved and underdeveloped. It wastes resources and limits our ministry, all under the guise of strong leadership and the use of our God-given talents for "getting things done." Robert Greenleaf reminds us that the difference between a true servant-leader who is servant first, and the leader-servant who seeks leadership first, lies in the growth of the people who serve under them. The test question is, "do those served grow as persons; do they, while being served, become healthier, wiser, freer, more autonomous, more likely themselves to become servants?"[18]

For this reason, leadership bent on increasing the leader lacks integrity. Integrity is the attribute of honesty, moral behavior and a value-centered life. Integrity witnesses externally all that we are internally. And for that reason, godly integrity begins with our inner life in God. Stephen Covey sees integrity as "the value we place on ourselves."[19] By that he means that we first must keep faith with ourselves if we are to be trusted and trustworthy to those around us. We must keep promises we make to our own value system. For the Christian leader this means that our self-confidence must be founded in our faith in Christ and our desire to be like Him in every way. We must seek to be Christlike in our inner being and be confident that "He who began a good work in you will be faithful to complete it" (Philippians 1:6). If Christ is truly living in us, as Paul reminds us, then we can in turn live for others in our work. We will have no need to seek for increase in our positions of power. We will have no desire to build our own kingdoms and advance our own reputations. Our lives are hidden with Christ in God (Colossians 3:3) and therefore it is no longer we who live, but Christ who lives in us (Galatians 2:20). It is only with this kind of godly integrity that we can seek to decrease as Christ increases in and through our work as leaders.

Truly godly leaders empower their people, give away authority, value and involve others, seek the best in and from their people, and constantly seek to lift others up, push others into the limelight, and reward those they lead. All so that God's will might be done in a more powerful way. They seek no glory for themselves, but find great joy in seeing others prosper. They take no account of their reputation, but seek that Jesus' face be seen in all they do. Max De Pree's famous definition is worth repeating, "The first responsibility of the leader is to define reality. The last is to say thank you. In between the leader is a servant."[20]

I have come to understand that godly leadership is a call to a lifestyle of an ever-decreasing thirst for authority, power and influence, where the quest for reputation is replaced by the power of God's anointing.

Being and Doing

I am a doer. I have the reputation of going 100+ mph always focused on accomplishing objectives, meeting time-lines and crossing things off my infamous "to-do" lists. I like results over process, action over deliberation, the tangible over the theoretical. And I like to lead people to accomplish goals and realize vision. What gets in my way are processes, people with "issues," using time inefficiently, and undertaking work that seems irrelevant. I am committed to transformation, as long as it can get done on schedule and show some real results.

The problem with this style of leadership is that is denies the truth of the gospel and our creation in the image of God. If we are truly made in the imago Dei, then our perception of God will significantly influence our own self-understanding. If we view God as a solitary Monad, an individual being known for His power and transcendence, then we will be leaders who reflect those characteristics. We will be lone rangers, seeking power and focusing on doing. We will see people as means to an end and value the product over the process. We will see relationships as tools for our productivity and community as an asset only when it contributes to the bottom line. This productivity model of leadership is the result of a conception of God as the sovereign, detached monarch. In that image, we lead as monarchs.

If, however, we are true to our Trinitarian historical commitments, we see instead a God who in His very nature is defined by relationship. We see Father, Son and Holy Spirit as distinct persons yet also interdependent in their perichoretic relationship. The mutual indwelling of the three persons of the Godhead gives us a different understanding of what God values in us and desires from us. Here we learn that relationship is what defines us. We learn that to be God's people we must focus on who we are as people in relationship. We learn that leadership must be concerned with the whole person, and that God's intent is for us to do the work of the kingdom within and through the community of believers.

All of this we come to know from only one place, namely, in the person of Jesus Christ. If our epistemological starting point is solely in the incarnation, life, death and resurrection of Jesus Christ, then our focus as leaders must change drastically. For Jesus was concerned about people over product, relationship over output, and transformation over transaction. And from beginning to end, Jesus was a servant.

We learn from a proper understanding of our creation in the imago Dei that what is most important to God is not what we do but who we are. Secular leadership experts are waking to the fact that the key to leadership effectiveness is self-awareness.[21] In Christian terms this means that the leader is transformed first!

Greenleaf recalls the story of a king who asked Confucius what to do about the large number of thieves. Confucius replied, "If you, sir, were not covetous, although you should reward them to do it, they would not steal." Greenleaf goes on to say, "This advice places an enormous burden on those who are favored by the rules, and it established how old is the notion that the servant views any problem in the world as in here, inside himself, and not out there. And if a flaw in the world is to be remedied, to the servant the process of change starts in here, in the servant, and not out there."[22]

Before God can do a great work in an organization, that work must be done first in the heart of the leader. And again this is especially true in Christian leadership. Unless God has taken our hearts captive, all of our good "doing" will lack spiritual integrity and authority. Our work will expose the absence of God's anointing. And it is at the exact moment that we think we "have it all together" that we cease to be useable in the work of the kingdom.

If I could put one Bible verse on the desk of every pastor and every Christian leader in the world it would be this, "If we say that we have no sin, we deceive ourselves and the truth is not in us" (1 John 1:8). As Christian leaders we must be engaged in a constant process of self-evaluation and repentance. It is so easy for us to be tempted in a variety of directions, and when we stray, we impact our entire ministry. Godly leaders undertake their work with a deep humility and a keen awareness of their own weaknesses and shortcomings. They know themselves well, seek accountability, pray fervently and watch carefully for red flags and warning signals. Nouwen challenges us to seek this central and defining characteristic of Christian leadership, "The central question [of the heart of Christian leadership] is, are the leaders of the future truly men and women of God, people with an ardent desire to dwell in God's presence, to listen to God's voice, to look at God's beauty, to touch God's incarnate Word, and to taste fully God's infinite goodness?"[23] For this reason, the greatest tool for effective Christian leadership may be a mirror, and a group of friends to be sure you are looking into it with clarity and focus.

Becoming a leader of no reputation means not being afraid to stare down your weaknesses and uncover the messy stuff in your private world. It means letting God transform you. And more importantly, it means knowing how much you need that transformation, far more than anyone else in your organization. I have come to understand the development of self-awareness and personal transformation as a critical aspect of Christian leadership. When this ongoing transformation is added to the desire to decrease while Christ increases, all under the anointing power of the Spirit, the Christian leader begins to emerge.

Leadership Is a Miracle

One of the greatest gifts I received during my term as president came from my colleague Ron Sider in the form of a book entitled,

"Leadership Prayers" by Richard Kriegbaum. The honesty and humility in these prayers bear witness to the heart of a godly leader. In his prayer for trust, Kriegbaum offers these words,

> I love you, God. You know I do. How natural it is to love you. You are perfect. You are beautiful, pure, powerful, absolutely truthful, and kind. You have been so generous to me that just saying thank you seems pitiful sometimes. But far more powerful in my life is knowing and feeling that you love me. You know exactly and completely who I am—all my ugly thoughts, my mangled motivations, my pretending, my irrational fears, my pride, and my unfaithfulness—and you still love me. *I know you love me. You know me, and yet, because you love me, you let me lead others. I do not understand it, but I am grateful.*[24]

In reading these words back through the lenses of my experience I have come to the conclusion that when God uses any of us to lead effectively, it is nothing short of a miracle. When we place the complex and demanding role of a godly leader next to an honest self-awareness of our own sinfulness and incompetence, we are thrown wholly upon the grace of God and His faithfulness if we are ever to lead anyone anywhere.

There is a corollary here to the miracle that occurs in both the efficacy of Scripture and in the effectiveness of our preaching. In both, human words are taken up by the power of the Holy Spirit to become the words of God. In both its inspiration and its interpretation, the words of Scripture are completely reliant on the activity of the Spirit of God. When the Spirit illumines the human word, hearts are changed, people are transformed and God's work is done. The same is true in our preaching. We study and prepare as we are trained to do, but in the end, our preaching only becomes effective when the Spirit of God takes up our feeble human words and uses them to touch hearts and change lives. When it happens it is a miracle!

Conversely, when we seek to have the written words of Scripture or the spoken words of the preacher stand alone apart from the work of the Spirit, our ministry loses its power. It becomes our words, our interpretation, our exegesis and our proclamation. And slowly and naturally into these words of ours will seep the ugly thoughts, mangled motivations, pretending, irrational fears, pride and unfaithfulness of Kriegbaum's prayer.

I have come to learn that we must approach leadership in dependent humility. Throughout history God looked to the least, the weakest, the outcast, the untalented, the sinful and the rejected to give great leadership at historic times. And He hasn't changed that approach today. If we are honest as leaders, we know that we are not capable of leading as the size and complexity of our call demands. We know that there are others more talented, more prepared, more spiritual and more courageous than are we. But great godly leaders have always worked at that miraculous intersection where humility and faith meet the awesome presence and power of God's Spirit. And the miracle of leadership happens. It doesn't mean that we don't prepare ourselves, hone our skills and seek to be the best we can be for the kingdom. What it does mean is that in the end, all that we bring will fall woefully short of what is required, and we will be ever thrown again into the grace and faithfulness of God to work the miracle of leadership in and through and even in spite of our small pile of skills and talents.

When God uses us to lead, and lead effectively, we should fall on our knees in wonder and thanksgiving that we have seen again this miracle worked in our midst. However, it is far too easy for us to take ownership of this miracle and to believe that these results are due to our own wonderful abilities and leadership qualities. If and when we make this subtle yet devastating shift, the efficacy of our leadership for the kingdom is over. We are on our own, cut off from the power and preservation of the Spirit. Every leader finds himself or herself there at some point in their work, and it is a terrifying place to be!

Godly leadership is the miracle of God's use of our earthen vessels for the glorious work of His kingdom. To miss this miraculous aspect of leadership will threaten everything we do as leaders, and our office or study will be the most lonely place on earth. I have come to understand the miracle of godly leadership, and its connection with self-awareness, the need to decrease and the power of God's anointing.

Seeking the Right Applause

A bookmark of mine carries a thought that stayed with me throughout my term as president of Eastern Seminary. It reads, "It doesn't matter if the world knows, or sees or understands, the only applause we are meant to seek is that of nail-scarred hands." Leaders are exposed to opportunities to generate applause. It can come in the form of commendation from the board, approval of our decisions by employees, recognition of our institution's work by constituencies, admiration of our leadership abilities by co-workers, and words of appreciation from students.

As public figures, we receive both the undue criticism for the failures of our institutions, and the unmerited praise for their successes. The true calling of leadership requires us to accept the former and deflect the latter. That is, our job is to take the blame for mistakes made by those under our leadership and to deflect the praise and re-direct it to those most responsible for our success. In this way we keep ourselves in balance, never taking the criticism too personally and not accepting the praise too easily. But this balance is often very difficult to maintain.

One axiom of leadership I have come to appreciate reads, "leaders do not inflict pain, they bear it." In the same manner, leaders do not absorb praise, they re-direct it. The success of any Christian leader lies significantly in their ability to keep this twofold movement of leadership in balance. Leaders who inflict pain lose trust and dishearten their people. Leaders who absorb praise produce resentment and sacrifice motivation.

Returning to where we began, this is why God's anointing is so important to the Christian leader. Only with God's anointing can the leader listen intently for that one source of applause that really matters. Only anointed leaders truly "seek first the kingdom of God and His righteousness." If we seek our affirmation elsewhere, the distracting noises that vie for our attention and tug at our hearts for allegiance will drown out all else. And if we seek for this other applause, we will never hear the one from the Master's hands.

Two significant temptations come to play here. The first is the fear of rejection that causes us to run from confrontation. The second is the desire to make everyone happy and to measure our performance, our effectiveness and our "leadership" on that scale. The two are very closely related. The first temptation is motivated by the idea that good leaders will not generate conflict, and that rejection of our performance in our role as leader is a rejection of our personhood and character. These are significant pitfalls for a leader. They are generated from that deep-seated desire to hear the applause of all with whom we work.

The second temptation is to lead by reacting. We see which way the wind is blowing and steer that direction, regardless of the situation. We do not want our people to be anxious, to question our decisions or disagree with our reasoning. We want harmony and unity, which is commendable. But left unchecked, this desire will cause us to sacrifice courage, vision and risk-taking. It will bring us momentary applause, but will ruin us in the end. To use a variation on a quote from Ralph Waldo Emerson, "Some leaders worry themselves into nameless graves, while here and there some forget themselves into immortality."

So we must ask ourselves just what kind of applause are we seeking? If it is human applause that validates, that affirms and that encourages us, we will also find that same applause binds us, boxes us in and ultimately strangles the life out of us. When our daily self-worth and the measure of our effectiveness come primarily from the reaction of those with whom we work, then we are finished as Christian leaders.

I was always amazed at how many decisions I was called upon to make in any given day; some in private, some in meetings and some in the public arena. Every day there were multiple opportunities to make "applause-generating" decisions. And sometimes the temptations to make them were enormous, especially when considering the price that would be paid if other alternatives were chosen. However, I was equally amazed at how often God's will and following His word took me down a different path. It is at that intersection between doing what God was telling us to do vs. doing the expedient and popular that true leadership takes place. It is there that we know to whom we are looking for our affirmation.

The goal of the Christian leader must be to go to bed every night with a clear conscience and a right heart with God. God only asks one thing of leaders, that we seek with all our heart to know and do His will.

Before taking on my leadership position I spent a couple of hours with a man whom I respect for his wisdom and leadership abilities. He gave me encouragement and good advice, and before I left he told me something that both inspires and haunts me to this day. He said, "Scott, in whatever you do, always strive to be a man that God can trust." I now believe that a man or woman that God can trust is one who seeks only the applause of nail-scarred hands. It is also one for whom the cultivation of reputation carries no value.

I did not have a clear understanding of this need for balance in the life of a Christian leader, and I have come to see it as an essential component for leadership in the kingdom of God.

Leadership in Transformation

My five years in the presidency is a study in transformation. I came in with a wrong set of expectations, values and ideas about Christian leadership. I was not thirsty for power or obsessed with the trappings of leadership, but I also was not seeking to be leader of no reputation, nor was I responding to the call because I was a servant first. And it was here that I was wrong.

I used to reject the notion that good Christian leaders were only those who were brought kicking and screaming into the position. Or that anyone who "wanted" to be a president should be automatically disqualified. I still believe that God prepares people for His work, and some aspects of this approach are not in keeping with our giftedness. However, the truth in this view is that servant leaders are servants first, and only as true servants are they called to lead. For those who see themselves as leaders first, these temptations to stray in leadership are enormous. "The long painful history of the Church is the history of people ever and again tempted to choose power over love, control over the cross, being a leader over being led. Those who resisted this temptation to the end and thereby give us hope are the true saints."[25]

I have left my years in the presidency with a dramatically transformed understanding of godly leadership, and one that continues to be transformed today. In the end, our work as leaders is all about lordship. Before it is about vision-casting or risk-taking or motivating others or building teams or communicating or strategic planning or public speaking, it is about lordship. Where Jesus is singularly and absolutely lord of our life, we will seek to be like Him and Him only. That will be our sole calling. We will be called to our work and that work will carry God's anointing. We will be called to decrease that Christ may increase. We will be called to be people of God before and as we do the work of God. We will be called to pray and look for the miracle of leadership that God may work in our midst. And we will be called to strain our ears for that one sweet sound of two nail-scarred hands affirming all that we do in His name.

In these ways, in responding faithfully to this calling and striving after these ideals at the cost of everything else that may tempt us, we become leaders. And as we do, we will be transformed into the likeness of Christ, becoming leaders of no reputation.

R. Scott Rodin is the former president of Eastern Baptist Theological Seminary, Philadelphia, Pennsylvania. He now serves as president of Rodin Consulting of Spokane, Washington, and part of the John R. Frank Consulting Group of Seattle, Washington.

Appendix B

Classic books recommended by Ken Boa (list used with permission):

1. *The Great Divorce* by C.S. Lewis
2. *Pensées* by Blaise Pascal
3. *The Knowledge of the Holy* by A.W. Tozer
4. *Confessions* by St. Augustine
5. *Mere Christianity* by C.S. Lewis
6. *The Sacrament of the Present Moment* by Jean-Pierre De Caussade
7. *The Brothers Karamazov* by Fyodor Dostoyevsky
8. *Frankenstein* by Mary Shelly
9. *The Pursuit of God* by A.W. Tozer
10. *Great Expectations* by Charles Dickens
11. *Pride and Prejudice* by Jane Austen
12. *The Return of the Prodigal Son* by Henri Nouwen
13. *Perelandra* by C.S. Lewis
14. *Crime and Punishment* by Fyodor Dostoyevsky
15. *The Imitation of Christ* by Thomas à Kempis
16. *Dracula* by Bram Stoker
17. *Robinson Crusoe* by Daniel Defoe
18. *Hamlet* by Shakespeare
19. *Othello* by Shakespeare
20. *King Lear* by Shakespeare
21. *The Screwtape Letters* by C.S. Lewis
22. *Pilgrim's Progress* by John Bunyan

23. *Paradise Lost* by John Milton

24. *Les Misérables* by Victor Hugo

25. *Dark Night of the Soul* by St. John of the Cross

26. *Anna Karenina* by Leo Tolstoy

27. *The Cost of Discipleship* by Dietrich Bonhoeffer

28. *East of Eden* by John Steinbeck

29. *Faust* by Johann Wolfgang von Goethe

30. *Institutes of the Christian Religion* by John Calvin

31. *The City of God* by Augustine

32. *Middlemarch* by George Eliot

33. *Moby Dick* by Herman Melville

34. *My Utmost for His Highest* by Oswald Chambers

35. *Orthodoxy* by G.K. Chesterton

36. *The Problem of Pain* by C.S. Lewis

37. *Religious Affections* by Jonathan Edwards

38. *A Serious Call to a Devout and Holy Life* by William Law

39. *Christian Perfection* by François Fénelon

40. *The Divine Comedy* by Dante Alighieri

41. *The Love of God* by Bernard of Clairvaux

42. *Fear and Trembling* by Søren Kierkegaard

43. *The Complete English Poems* by George Herbert

44. *That Hideous Strength* by C.S. Lewis

45. *The Odyssey* by Homer

46. *The Iliad* by Homer

About the Author

B oyd Bailey is the president of the National Christian Foundation in Georgia. His passion is to love leaders and help them grow in their journey of generosity with Jesus.

Since 2004, he has also served as president and founder of Wisdom Hunters, a ministry that connects people to Christ through devotional writings, with more than 150,000 daily followers by email, social media, podcast, and the Wisdom Hunters app.

In 1999, Boyd cofounded Ministry Ventures, which has trained leaders in approximately 1,000 faith-based nonprofits, and coached for certification more than 200 ministries in the best practices of prayer, board development, ministry model, administration, and fund-raising. By God's grace, these ministries have raised more than $100 million, and thousands of people have been led into growing relationships with Jesus Christ.

Prior to Ministry Ventures, Boyd was the national director for Crown Financial Ministries. He was instrumental in the expansion of Crown into 30 major markets across the United States. He was a key facilitator in the $25 million merger between Christian Financial Concepts and Crown Financial Ministries.

Before his work with Crown, Boyd, with Andy Stanley, started First Baptist of Atlanta's north campus. As an elder, Boyd also assisted Andy in the start of North Point Community Church.

Boyd received a Bachelor of Arts from Jacksonville State University and a Master of Divinity from Southwestern Seminary in Fort Worth, Texas. Boyd and his wife, Rita, live in Roswell, Georgia. They have been married 38 years and are blessed with four daughters, four sons-in-law, and seven grandchildren.

WISDOM
HUNTERS

H e who walks with wise men will be wise, but the companion of fools will suffer harm" (Proverbs 13:20 NASB).

In 2003, Boyd Bailey began to informally email personal reflections from his morning devotional time to a select group of fellow wisdom hunters. Over time, these informal emails grew into Wisdom Hunters Daily Devotional. Today, thanks to God's favor and faithful followers, these emails and social media posts reach more than 150,000 readers each day.

Boyd remains relentless in the pursuit of wisdom and continues to daily write raw, original, real-time reflections from his personal encounters with the Lord.

Visit www.WisdomHunters.com where you can:

- Subscribe to free daily devotional emails
- Find out how to access our blog, Facebook, Twitter, Instagram, and the new Wisdom Hunters podcast
- Choose from a wide selection of devotional books on marriage, wisdom, wise living, and money; with books also for graduates, fathers, mothers, and more (eBook and print versions available)
- Download the free Wisdom Hunters app for Apple and Android

The thoughtful comments and wisdom our followers share each day can help us all in our journey with God.

National Christian
FOUNDATION®

Founded in 1982 and based in Atlanta, Georgia, the National Christian Foundation (NCF) is a charitable giving ministry that provides wise giving solutions, mobilizes resources, and inspires biblical generosity for Christian families, advisors, and charities. NCF is currently the ninth-largest US nonprofit, having accepted more than $9 billion in contributions. It has granted more than $7 billion to more than 40,000 charities. The NCF Giving Fund, or donor-advised fund, allows donors to make charitable contributions and then recommend grants to the charities they care about, over time. NCF is also an industry leader in accepting gifts of appreciated assets, such as stocks, real estate, and business interests, which enables donors to save on taxes and align their charitable goals with their family, business, estate, and legacy plans. Learn more about NCF at www.NCFgiving.com.

More Great Harvest House
Books by Boyd Bailey

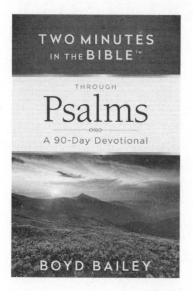

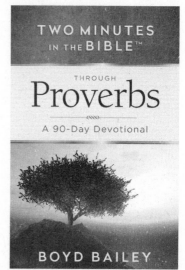

TWO MINUTES
IN THE BIBLE™

FOR
Women
A 90-Day Devotional

SHANA SCHUTTE
WITH BOYD BAILEY

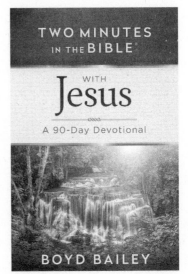

TWO MINUTES
IN THE BIBLE®

WITH
Jesus
A 90-Day Devotional

BOYD BAILEY

TWO MINUTES
IN THE BIBLE®

THROUGH
Revelation
A 90-Day Devotional

BOYD BAILEY

Notes

1. Charles Spurgeon, "The Fourfold Treasure," a message given on Thursday evening, April 27, 1871, at the Metropolitan Tabernacle. See at http://www.romans45.org/spurgeon/sermons/0991.htm.

2. C.S. Lewis, *Mere Christianity* (New York: Collier Books, 1952), p. 114.

3. Lewis, *Mere Christianity*.

4. Rick Warren, Twitter post, October 22, 2014.

5. See at http://lifeequip.com/leadership-development/leadership-tips-why-successful-leadership-needs-love/.

6. "George Herbert's Love," see at https://prezi.com/y806jsaxjtyp/george-herberts-love/.

7. Merriam-Webster's Collegiate Dictionary, 11th ed., s.v. "discipline."

8. See at https://tadhgtalks.me/2016/08/18/acornology-the-story-of-the-acorn/.

9. See at https://www.goodreads.com/work/quotes/26961849-soul-keeping-caring-for-the-most-important-part-of-you.

10. See at https://nfcchelp.org.

11. See at http://www.afriprov.org/african-stories-by-season/14-animal-stories/67-how-the-monkeys-saved-the-fish.html.

12. See at www.givewithjoy.org.

13. See at https://greatergood.berkeley.edu/forgiveness/definition.

14. See at http://annvoskamp.com/2012/05/for-the-days-that-seem-to-be-going-bad. Note that this story was also cited by Max Lucado, and may have its origins in South America.

15. Henri Nouwen, *In the Name of Jesus* (New York: Crossroads, 1996), 17.

16. John Adams in David McCullough, *John Adams* (New York: Simon & Schuster, 2001), 19.

17. Nouwen, *In the Name of Jesus*, 62-63.

18. Robert K. Greenleaf, *The Servant as Leader* (Newton Center: Greenleaf Center, 1970), 7.

19. Stephen R. Covey, *Principle-Centered Leadership* (New York: Fireside, 1990), 61.

20. James O'Toole, *Leading Change* (New York: Ballantine Books, 1995), 44.

21. Among the many authors who are championing the cause of careful self-awareness are James O'Toole, Stephen Covey, Noel Tichy, John Kotter, Peter Block, Warren Bennis, Max DePree, and Peter Drucker.

22. Greenleaf, *The Servant as Leader*, 34.

23. Nouwen, *In the Name of Jesus*, 29-30.

24. Richard Kriegbaum, *Leadership Prayers* (Wheaton, IL: Tyndale House, 1998), 22 (italics mine).

25. Nouwen, 60.